Encounters in Thought

Encounters in Thought

Beyond Instrumental Reason

AARON K. KERR

 CASCADE *Books* · Eugene, Oregon

ENCOUNTERS IN THOUGHT
Beyond Instrumental Reason

Cascade Books
An Imprint of Wipf and Stock Publishers
199 W. 8th Ave., Suite 3
Eugene, OR 97401

www.wipfandstock.com

PAPERBACK ISBN: 978-1-5326-3916-6
HARDCOVER ISBN: 978-1-5326-3917-3
EBOOK ISBN: 978-1-5326-3918-0

Cataloguing-in-Publication data:

Names: Kerr, Aaron K., author.

Title: Encounters in thought : beyond instrumental reason / Aaron K. Kerr.

Description: Eugene, OR: Cascade Books, 2019 | Includes bibliographical references and index.

Identifiers: ISBN 978-1-5326-3916-6 (paperback) | ISBN 978-1-5326-3917-3 (hardcover) | ISBN 978-1-5326-3918-0 (ebook)

Subjects: LCSH: Education—Philosophy | Reasoning (psychological) | Knowledge, Theory of (Religion) | Anselm, Saint, Archbishop of Canterbury, 1033–1109 | Saulitis, Eva, 1963–2016 | Merton, Thomas, 1915–1968 | X, Malcolm,—1925–1965 | Imagination (Philosophy) | Critical thinking

Classification: LB1025.2 K27 2019 (paperback) | LB1025.2 (ebook)

Manufactured in the U.S.A.   10/14/19

For Gretchen, partner in the search for cool, clear water

Contents

Preface

WHAT DO AN ELEVENTH-CENTURY Archbishop, a twenty-first-century marine biologist and poet, a mid-twentieth-century hermit and a mid-twentieth-century global revolutionary for racial justice have in common? St. Anselm, Eva Saulitis, Thomas Merton, and Malcolm X found the potential and range of their intellects at the very point when they said no to the conventional patterns set for them by family, education, culture, and society. All four made keen discoveries in their respective orbits of life and work. All four took those discoveries seriously in order to mine these insights for the world around them. All four of them integrated their mind and heart, and thus amplified and actualized the powers of their reason. They are most alike, however, in the way each of them lived out the moral implications of their hard-won beliefs and as their lives unfolded, those implications were embodied, demonstrating clearly a new order of value. And of course they are featured as the centerpiece of four chapters in this book because they demonstrate the fusion of intellectual and moral virtue. That integration seems in short supply these days.

What if you were able to rinse your mind once in a while? What if you could put your mind through a process in which the lesser grit and parasitical ideas that lived somewhere among your dendrites could be washed away? The rinse would be like the way a stunning rock traveling long in the patterns of the waves' crashing has finally been exposed by a riptide; now gleaming there just for your observations. Water is a fine analog here. To rinse your mind the way you rinse a greasy cast-iron skillet without soap in order to insure the iron remains seasoned for future flavoring. What ideas, specks of thought, or globs of speculation would you rinse away first? What patterns and wavelengths, crashing patterns of thought, keep the gems buried in froth and sand; moved by forces we seem unable to halt?

Persons who have learned to rinse their minds are persons who have learned how to renew their thinking through a certain enjoyment of reason classically construed as wonder, but perhaps parsed out in more detailed analysis as openness, wonder, receptivity, and contemplation. These classic dispositions of philosophical and theological discovery can serve as a sort of rinsing process, but first they must be understood, then they must be exemplified, and third they must be applied, or practiced in an intentional way, which admits of the struggle and confusion often involved in intellectual, moral, and spiritual searching. After an introductory essay, each chapter of this book invites persons to understand something of the structure of their mind's patterns in light of a *description* of openness, wonder, receptivity, and contemplation. A description is followed by an exemplar, someone who has taught us incisively about intellectual transformation. That *exemplification* is followed by a practice through which openness, wonder, receptivity, and contemplation might *apply*. Since our contemporary context demands that we re-think or even re-situate our human competence as stewards of the earth, the last chapter explores *water* as an elemental, running it through our open minds, wondering about what it is, how it has been received, and contemplating its essential and inestimable value.

What if we taught our children with the rinsing process at hand? That would mean we would have to interrupt their digital learning patterns, but their enjoyment of learning may increase exponentially over time. Innovators and collaborators have certain moral and intellectual dispositions that can be cultivated early on. These dispositions are necessary for a full life, a life of truth and authenticity. But they take patience and practice. Patience in learning is weakened by digital culture. And the practices discussed here are deemed unnecessary today because of the value of convenience, which tends to weaken curiosity. All manner of people worry a lot about the fragmentation of society, the inability for academic disciplines to understand one-another, but those people often fail to take stock of the technological practices to which all of us are beholden. We thus give up on understanding truth in its many profiles: scientifically, religiously, and philosophically. Those profiles fit together and broaden our vision, but we never take the time necessary to put them all together. Our lives are cut in a pattern that forms our thinking: thinking *more and more about less and less*. Rather than rinse, we are drowning in distraction. That noise blocks our reason because it keeps us from encounters: with others, nature, and God. What follows is an invitation to re-encounter your own mind, the Western philosophical tradition, truth, nature, and perhaps the Spirit.

This book is set within two over-arching concerns of our time. It can be opened by a question. What is the relation between the urgent need for a deep ecology and the burgeoning moral implications of media ecology? The media ecology is the frenetic digital pattern through which and in which we find information and meaning. A deep ecology is a conscious movement toward those political and regional efforts to preserve and conserve nature precisely because nature's value has been discerned; it is a deep awareness. The media ecology, the fruit of the technological pattern started in the eighteenth century, carries on by forming and stretching the consumptive society that forged the degradation of nature through industrialization. If we do not interrogate our technological culture we remain distracted in digital patterns of consumerism. Our relationship to nature or water cannot be interrupted or changed as long as we presume that we can forego our relationships to teachers or the wisdom of the past. All our learning is relational in some aspect. What follows aims at a renewal of that aspect through encounter, encounters in thought; I encountered a reader in my imagination when I wrote these words. My hope is that reading through this book will give you a novel way forward, beyond instrumental reason.

Acknowledgements

LIGHT COMES FROM EVERYWHERE. I am grateful for two upper-level philosophy students, Dan Kaufman and Michael Laher. They took a *Philosophy of Place* travel course with me and then became embedded tutors in first-year philosophy classes in the fall of 2018. The travel course was designed with the support of Gannon's Barker Globalization grant, and has paid out great learning dividends. Mike and Dan helped me to understand student experience and their dedication to thinking and encouragement was especially gratifying. I am very grateful for the insights of Meredith LaFontaine and Craig Whipkey, two master teachers who have been able to enlist their creativity in the classroom while understanding the vital necessity of digital technology in contemporary pedagogy. I met them through chance encounters, Meredith at a conference at Notre Dame and Craig at a wonderful wedding celebration held out of doors. Those encounters got me to thinking and I wanted to understand more about their creative work as teachers. Their thought and practice serve as the entry point to the argument of this book. I have been inspired by my work with Inter-Church Ministries of Erie County, especially the executive director, Diane Edwards and the president Johnny Johnson. They are leading the city of Erie in conversations about white privilege and institutional racism, which has brought us to difficult conversations, but redemptive light shines through. I am encouraged and edified by my colleagues in the philosophy department at Gannon University: Stephanie Barnhizer, Bill Haggerty, David Nordquest, Dominic Prianti, Mike Latzer, and Fr. Jason Mitchell. Theologians at Gannon, particularly Eric Dart and Fr. Casimir Wozniak, have also discussed the questions this book pursues with me for the past few years. Fr. Jerome Simmons continues to guide me in the craft of listening to the Spirit, I am grateful for such a rowdy and insightful friend. Retired math teacher Russell Campbell helped me to formulate and symbolize the quadratic encounter in receptivity and he and his wife Ellen have been so receptive to me over many years of friendship. Thanks to Fr. Philip Oriole who suggested I read Walter Isaacson's biography of da Vinci. I have had great administrative support from Sabine Preuss-Miller, who worked on the bibliography. I am especially grateful to be working with my colleagues in the college of Humanities, Education, and Social Sciences at Gannon University: CHESS. Dean Linda Fleming has consistently invited the faculty to address learning needs that have come as a result of digital culture, notably a re-tooling in information literacy and fluency. Education professor Robin Quick and research librarian Emmett Lombard have been very instructive by helping me to understand the context of reading and digital research respectively. Ongoing discussions with political science professor Mark Jubulis, social work professor Parris Baker, criminal justice professor Chris Magno, and president of Winebrenner Theological Seminary, Brent Sleasman, broadened my scope. Special thanks to English professor Carol Hayes, who read portions of the manuscript and made helpful suggestions and corrections. I am especially blessed to occupy an office next to philosopher Mike Latzer, who, in addition to his quick and caring wit, provides a listening ear and a loving heart to all who stand at his door. He read over the chapter on contemplation and made helpful suggestions. In addition to these encounters in thought, I owe a heaping debt of gratitude to Pat O'Connell. This English and theology professor, a Merton scholar, has been so generous with his time, his vast knowledge, and his resources. He read the whole manuscript and pointed me in the right direction, with the right question at just the right time. Also, my good friend Bill Hunter, outdoor planner at the National Park Service, has been a consistent conversation partner of foresight and insight for twenty-nine years. Some of his voice may have mixed with mine in the words herein. None of my work as a philosopher, father, or friend, however, would be of any meaning to me or anyone else for that matter were it not for Gretchen Hall. She has been my partner in openness, wonder, receptivity, and contemplation for a long while. I dedicate this book to her.

1

Guidance beyond Convenience and Distraction

"How proud we often are of our victories in the war with nature, proud of the multitude of instruments we have succeeded in inventing, of the abundance of commodities we have been able to produce. Yet our victories have come to resemble defeats. In spite of our triumphs, we have fallen victims to the work of our hands; it is as if these forces we had conquered have conquered us."

—Abraham Joshua Heschel

In the Summer of 2011, two philosophers and a community farmer had a conversation around a table at Betty's Bed and Breakfast in Missoula, Montana. They had a lot to talk about, since the two philosophers were experts in the ethics of sustainable agriculture and the culture of technology respectively, and the farmer had developed a transformative farming experiment that connects alienated youth and low-income senior citizens together in food production and consumption.[1] Farmer Josh Slotnick, who sat with his back to the video camera, seemed to be living out the teachings of these insightful thinkers; provoked, perhaps, by his experience of

1. Paul Thompson, Professor of Agriculture, Food, and Community Ethics, Michigan State University, Albert Borgmann, Regents Professor of Philosophy, University of Montana, and Josh Slotnick, community organizer and farmer at Peas Farm in Montana. https://www.youtube.com/watch?v=1O_cBJCpQYA.

working with "troubled" youth, the community farmer proposed that in the culture at large there are "high production expectations" for young adults. The philosopher of culture, Albert Borgmann, took up this theme and asked a question that has been with me ever since. It is a question I take into the classrooms with me, a question at the forefront of my fatherhood, and a question through which I recognize my own formative struggles with the meaning of life and success. The question is: "Why do the best and the brightest in our culture make their lives miserable?" Borgmann elaborates by asking us to imagine we have a really smart daughter who goes to Harvard, then Yale Law School, and then gets hired on at a law firm in New York City and starts out at $200,000 a year. But then he says something that interrupts this conventional narrative of pride. He says, "If that happens, your heart has to sink, because her life is going to be miserable." Miserable? How so? She has pursued and is now living the dream! Upon reflection, we all see that he is right. If you commit to that level of success, your life will be consumed with production, working at least seventy hours a week. If you don't work seventy hours a week, guess what: you will be replaced in an awful hurry, despite your great credentials and your wicked smart pedigree. The YouTube label to this particular video segment is *How did misery become our goal?* Borgmann suggests that only 20 percent of the population will have these high-production expectations. But he also suggests that the rest of the population is expected to "consume, consume, consume." In order to be such a consumer, we are told we must have some form of education and so the drive to become employable is riven with the singular pressures of competition. And strangely, I have found that "the best and the brightest" that find their way to a small Catholic university in Northwestern Pennsylvania, are, on average, not as creative and open as those average students who sit in the same classrooms with them. I sense in the "best and brightest" a rigidity of mind that I have concluded has something to do with the obsession with grades, and learning how to get high marks, rather than learning content, or how to think about the content. If Borgmann, Slotnick, and Thompson are correct, and misery has become the goal (or at least the result) and the persons who go after that goal are the smartest among us, why do we persist in this misery? To what are we beholden?

It depends on what kind of philosopher you ask. We are beholden to assumptions of modernity, Western hegemony, individualism, fifteen minutes of fame, global capitalism, racism, sexism, greed, intransigent political ideology, religious or humanistic dogma, or some collusion between all these realities. These all deserve our careful attention, but there is something hidden from view and much more commonplace that has come to the surface more forcefully with digital devices. This leads me to the second question Albert Borgmann has asked that also haunts my teaching and writing. Borgmann is probably the most well-known philosopher of technology North America has. Theologians and spiritual writers have offered commentaries that contextualize especially his significant contribution to ethics, the focal practices. We would do well to think about the fruit of his thirty-year analysis of what he calls the *device paradigm*.

Put simply, the device paradigm is the moral pattern of engagement formed by technological development. Its results are convenience, ease of consumption, the compression of space and time, and the slow erosion of the symmetry between us and the way things are. Take a college course syllabus, for example. Over the past three years I have noticed two things. First, students now treat the syllabus as optional, and secondly, fail to retain information and concepts they have already looked up on the online version of the syllabus. Digital access means that we approach things as *data*, not necessarily as what they actually are—in the case of syllabi, as documents. Existing online, the syllabus is always accessible to students at any time. Because it is always there, it presents itself not as a whole to be carefully examined and read in one sitting, but rather as a collection of snippets. It is consulted when students have questions about what books they might get out of the library or buy, when exams take place, the weighting of assessments, or the length of a paper. If the student is not forewarned about certain vital aspects of information in the syllabus, he or she may not think it necessary to look at it. The instructor, who may have developed the syllabus over a period of, say, five years, presents it as a coherent contractual document of learning; a document that not only has necessary information, but also invites students into a set of agreements by which they are bound to particular events of learning and other actual moments of assessment. The syllabus is not a menu. The paradigm of accessibility that online engagement forms carries the expectation that the syllabus is full of data and there at hand to give whatever it is I happen to need at the time. Less and less is the syllabus understood as a document to be read in a particular context. No longer a preface to deep learning in a classroom environment for fifteen weeks of one's life, it is absorbed piecemeal like a mid-day snack. As Borgmann has said in so many other ways, the paradigm "degrades the symmetry between humanity and reality."[2] This pattern works for us and on us. It involves disburdenment and detachment. These are Borgmann's words. Let's put it more stringently: the device pattern makes us reliant on the pleasures derived from its efficiency and convenience; and it fragments us from the context out of which the commodity was produced. Searching for information on a syllabus online detaches us from the context of its native environment (the classroom) and fragments the coherence of the syllabus itself when we scroll looking only for due dates. Students now are reading written texts the same way. Perhaps they always have to an extent, but reading now seems a series of quick scans, looking for words in order to find the most important words, and these most important words are the data possessed for an assessment. *Searching* has lost its variable, manifold, and existential depth. Now, let's move onto Borgmann's second question.

In a 2001 essay, "Information, Nearness, and Farness," Borgmann considers the moral implications of the device pattern for food production and consumption.[3] Always accessible, efficiently produced and marketed food has worsened food quality overall for the past eighty years.[4] Accessibility has led to hyper-consumption. The ironic result is that the poorest among us are the most obese. One could begin to argue that highly accessible and cheaply made foods are a public health danger. Here is the question Borgmann's analysis elicits: if the device paradigm in the industrial age of food production has led to obesity, what will the device paradigm in the digital age lead to? I asked some of the "best and brightest" that question and here are a few of their answers.[5]

- Isolation
- Stupidity
- Ignorance
- Disconnectedness
- Laziness

2. Borgmann, "Reflections and Reviews," 420.

3. Borgmann, "Information, Nearness, and Farness," 104.

4. Food safety has certainly improved, but large-scale production has weakened foods' taste and other qualities.

5. These were the responses of an Honors Ethics class in the fall of 2015. I had lectured on Borgmann's device paradigm and asked them the question, this was after mid-term and they were beginning to interrupt their own presumptions regarding convenience and efficiency.

- Greed
- Narcissism
- Lethargy
- De-sensitization

These two questions—why do the best and brightest make their lives miserable? and if the device paradigm of the industrial age led to obesity, what will it lead to in the digital age?—both reveal that those at the top and those in poverty are impacted negatively by systems of power that do not interrogate the moral meaning of the digital pattern. As Borgmann has suggested, technology is a cultural force. But the paradigm's force must be understood, appreciated, and then creatively engaged. "Encounters in thought" are moral necessities for that very reason; they are ways to creatively approach the indispensability and ubiquity of digital technology while renewing the vitality and enjoyment of reason. Many have addressed the problem of digital life, and Borgmann has done so sufficiently because he offers what he calls focal practices as life-giving alternatives to digital emptiness. Focal practices produce encounters in thought. It is now time to cultivate these alternatives that both encourage and edify.

Our digital searching leaves us dissatisfied and often disagreeable. So encounters in thought are undertaken because, as Aristotle taught, we have both a cognitive ache for the truth, and a deep desire to know.[6] You might be thinking, "Well, it's fine for philosophers and farmers to think about these problems, but they remain protected from the daily digital engagements that are necessary for me to survive." That may be, but unless we interrupt the paradigm with our own reasonable practices, we remain mired in the debilitating technological determinism that redounds with either dystopian futures of robots taking vital signs in emergency rooms or utopian visions of living in a virtual paradise. There are caring and thoughtful educators who are doing creative interruptions to digital and instrumental patterns. I interviewed them to find out what they thought they were up against, and what they were doing about it in order to surmount the cultural force.

6. Aristotle, *Basic Works*, 689.

DIGITAL TRANSPOSITIONS

"Once they try it, they love it. Most of them rave about it, it is freeing for them."
—Meredith LaFontaine, JP II High School

"That part they always remember, that part they always thank us for, and they always have the highest marks for that time."
—Craig Whipkey, Central Valley High School

Meredith LaFontaine and Craig Whipkey teach high-school students. These quotes could well be snippets from ads for an educational product they swear by, perhaps an app that would enhance and bolster curricula. But what they are describing is hardly as convenient as buying a product; in fact, it may be everything that consumption and convenience are not: goals won only through the challenge of struggle. Relational, integrative, and sustaining. But what is the "it" to which Meredith refers, and what is the "part" Craig speaks of? Both the "it" and the "part" are what philosopher Albert Borgmann has called "focal practices." Before we discuss the significance and meaning of such practices, a bit more about Meredith LaFontaine and Craig Whipkey is in order, as well as the "it" and the "part" that has made all the difference in their classrooms and beyond.

THE DIGITAL TRANSPOSITION OF BOREDOM

Meredith LaFontaine teaches theology in a Catholic high school in Texas. She is responsible for teaching theology to 9–12 graders. In the past five to six years, she has seen the rise of digital technology as an *opportunity* to renew the experience and relevance of silence in the life of her students. In the quote above, silence is that to which "it" refers. But this insistence that students take time to be quiet has not been without her own persistent and arduous struggle with her students, and even colleagues. Meredith is not an "anti-technological Luddite," as we are wont to describe those who raise critical questions about technology. No, Meredith researches for her *Justice* class online; she agreed to be interviewed digitally for this introductory essay. She invites students, from time to time, to look up matters related to her classes on the iPads the school provides. But, like many of us in education and the helping professions, Meredith sees two moral problems with the ubiquity of devices in education, what we might call the digitization of the classroom.

The first has to do with students' interest and capacity to initiate their own learning. According to Meredith, more and more students want to be "spoon-fed," and "don't really want to work hard."[7] A second noticeable development has to do with what Meredith describes as a "reality vacuum" that sucks the students into a world in which the fourth dimension is compressed.[8] Related to the reality vacuum is the social media affect/effect. Put simply, "everything has to be super-relevant to their lives or they are not interested in it." If you are an educator or pastor, perhaps you have had similar experiences. Meredith shared: "When I moved to Texas and started teaching here, I encountered students talking while I was talking. When I confronted the students, one replied, 'If I don't see how it means anything to me then I just don't care.'" For every student who has the audacity to say something like that, think about how many of us live to some degree in that same economy of reasoning; but alas we keep our thoughts, as it were, to ourselves.

Acknowledging technology's positive uses, but also recognizing this particular historical moment, Meredith LaFontaine *forces* her students to be silent in class, and then invites students to go on retreat (this is optional) where they are away from their phones for hours at a time. This is what they love. "They rave about it, it is freeing for them." This book has something to do with re-entering that freedom, informed and conscious of its significance. Also, we intend to appreciate how that kind of loving is indispensable to living and learning well. The assumption is that, if we who educate are to lead others to intellectual self-trust and freedom, we must re-invigorate our own lives with intentional encounters in thought. When

7. Meredith LaFountaine in discussion with author, March 2018. All subsequent quotes by Meredith LaFountaine from that March discussion.

8. The fourth dimension, space-time, is analogous to dimensions one to three; length, width, and depth. One to three are how we experience space; through cyber-space, the fourth dimension is "traveled" since digitization compresses space and time, at least our experience of it. A student could be listening to a geometry lecture, but on her phone her mother, who is sitting in her office suite two hundred miles away, draws that student into that distant space and time by texting her a question or sending her a snap-chat of her new desk. Albert Borgmann critiques the value of living in the fourth dimension through cyber-space in his, "Digital Restlessness and Something More Certain."

asked about her own encounters with silence, Meredith simply says, "I was reared that way."[9]

Before creating the learning environment of silence, LaFontaine has had to analyze, diagnose, and articulate the problem to her students. Her research about her students' digital tendencies has led her to articulate clear expectations at the beginning of each school year. Unlike most other classrooms at a school that distributes iPads, she requires students to put away their devices in her class. They are only to be pulled out at her command, in order to look something up. "My class is associated with unplugging, I should never see your phone," she says.

She has seen a problem of culture where many of us see mere adolescent resistance, or worse, technological determinism. "My students cannot have their computers out and just stare at the wall. That is just miserable to them, their phone is just second nature, if their phone is out they are just going to engage with them." Also, she reports how stressed her students are. "These kids are extremely stressed out so they are very grateful for that silence, . . . not having to *do* anything, just being, not doing, being present and being there and not having to be responsible at that time." Anxiety, stress, distraction, and depression may be normative adolescent realities. One wonders, however, about the digital process of iPhones and iPads, and how the compressed fourth dimension intensifies these burdens. Certainly, we can appreciate "just being, not doing." When was last time, you, Dear Reader, stared at a wall? Though Meredith uses that as a euphemism for thinking without agenda, I like the image and the possibility.

When we look at paintings, are we not staring at the wall? When we stare at a blank wall there is so much going on. Some of it involves what St. Augustine calls *colligenda*, a bringing together of our memories to the perception of the wall. Do we not open out the multi-dimensional intricacies of thinking in this observation? If we really do observe the wall, we notice its cracks, consider its color, configure how a painting may hang, symmetrically or not, proportional to the corner of the room, or other imagined things that may be put on the wall. Our sense of proportion itself

9. The Latin, *Educare* and *Educere*, mean to bring up and to draw out, respectively. The former refers to raising children or fruit; the later refers to exiting, leading out. Both of these words contain *Ducere*: to lead, guide and direct. Parents are the most effective educators. But classroom teachers are leaders, and as leaders teachers must confront anything that gets in the way of the student's potential for thinking. As the rest of the book hopes to explore, we can own our capacity to lead our intellectual life, and with good teachers can be led to an open space of discovery where we enter the land for ourselves.

is collected either through previous perception of symmetry or innate mathematical senses, or likely a combination of both. "Nevertheless, the mind claims the verb cogitate for its own province. It is what is collected (that is, by force) in the mind, not elsewhere, which is strictly speaking the object of recollection."[10] The mind's potent force is animated by *collecting*, then *sorting*, then *adjudicating*. All this is, as St. Augustine testifies with astonishment, somewhere within. He settles on the soul and presents this beautiful metaphor, "No doubt, then, memory is, as it were, the stomach of the mind . . . ."[11] And in the mind, we also look for what is not there, for are we not inferring more about the wall that we just don't see. Its other side, inner structure? Better yet, when we stare at the wall, how often do we imagine the wall not being there at all? Perhaps we ought to consider the digital screen a wall, the wall between us and reality. LaFontaine is concerned that: "we are losing part of being human because we have this screen in between us and the world." With St. Augustine, we are concerned that we are not "moved to great astonishment" about the encounter with thought itself.[12] This is true of high-school students, but it is also true of my experience as a colleague and friend. A *meeting* is another word for encounter, but are we having a *meeting* if most of the participants are staring at the screens "between us"? LaFontaine suggests that this is an issue "even with people my age; it is definitely not just teenagers, [but] a lot of adults [too]. . . . Phones have made robots of so many people. . . . There is a pedigree of adults who have been looking for that forever, for cell phones, they want distraction." The digitization of culture means that in both youth and many adults the meaning and measurement of boredom are transposed.

What is it that is transposed? Boredom is a disposition of momentary seclusion after quickened intellectual stimulants. Our boredom is the aftermath, the self in isolation. Perhaps we are coming down from a great accomplishment, or likely, an expected event, purchase, or movie. Boredom is that dis-integration of coming down and the mild disgust involved in the realization that I still have this nagging need, this brooding desire for something. Or, boredom is simply that coming down and entering into a *day-dream*. There are many ways to parse Western boredom. Now it is a matter of generational aggregations of buying power leading to the confusion of wants and needs. Now it is the value of convenience unhinged from

10. Saint Augustine, *Confessions*, 189–90.
11. Saint Augustine, *Confessions*, 191.
12. Saint Augustine, *Confessions*, 187.

the value of the work of production. Now it is due to the media ecology rising from radio to TV to the ubiquitous internet. Now it is that inevitable biological fact, an innate tendency to search for the constituents of survival: food, mate, shelter. All these factors mitigate more meaningful and realistic truths about our lives. And alleviating boredom protects from the fact that most of us are average people who desire to be loved. Going digital is a relief from the bare encounter with a hollow silence. We search, and re-search for the stimulus that will acknowledge our presence. This move in the digitization of culture at once justifies and alleviates the cold abandon-ments of individualism. The hollow self hardly has a chance to enter the emptiness when the force of the "reality vacuum" pulls. For all of us in a digital culture, boredom is transposed into a bearable commercial jingle as the awkward silence of day-dreaming sheepishly dissipates. Boredom isn't given the chance to be the long two-beat-rest out of which an interesting melody is born.

By describing student boredom as misery LaFontaine recognizes the weight of digital culture but also sees how silence captures and eases ado-lescent anxiety. Sometimes this exercise moves outdoors as she encourages her students to "observe your surroundings, if there are ants, look at them!" Quoting Pope Francis, LaFontaine warns her students about "mental pol-lution," which cuts us off from "the great sages of the past." Being quiet outside the classroom enables the Catholic Social Teaching unit on *The Care for Creation* to speak to students in a more realistic and integral way.[13] By interrupting the digital pattern with silence and leaving the classroom environment, Meredith LaFontaine creates small openings for students to explore discretely their own consciousness. First, they have to encounter a teacher like Meredith, then they have to be open to their internal experi-ence, then their encounter with the outdoors broadens and deepens the encounter with silence. Of course, none of this can be measured according to the assessment techniques required at all levels of education today. With some good humor, LaFontaine has imagined what her colleagues think about these pedagogies. "I am sure they walk by my classroom and see us having silent time and think, 'Oh, there is theology doing nothing again.' People don't realize how important that is, to just sit, it is not a waste of your time!" Yet there is something quite poetic about the statement, *theology doing nothing again*. Faith and reason are intertwined in a buoyant repartee, and, being so carried away to float on still waters might make it appear

13. Pope Francis, *Laudato Si: On Care for Our Common Home*, 32, paras. 47–48.

that "nothing" is happening. Silence as a way to interrupt digital patterns has its place, but so do other types of engagements, especially for secondary students, for, as Craig Whipkey makes clear, high-school students are kinesthetic learners; perhaps that is why the iPad and phones are so enthusiastically utilized at this educational level.

THE DIGITAL TRANSPOSITION OF INSTRUCTION

Craig Whipkey teaches both biology and environmental science. Freshmen biology is a Pennsylvania state requirement and students take the Keystone exams to assess their biological learning. Whipkey and his colleagues' effectiveness as teachers is assessed in part by how well the freshmen biology students do on the Keystones (so called because of Pennsylvania's nickname, "the Keystone State"). Craig has a cadre of biology teachers who have developed the exact same content areas, on the exact same days, taught with the exact same examples and curriculum. Formatting biology this way is due exclusively to the test each student will have to take at the conclusion of the class. The biology teachers have agreed to this strict format "so that we get through all the material, so that there is no partiality on which teacher covers this longer than that, in order to maintain consistency and uniformity we have it all mapped out for a full year, same material, same lessons, pretty much in the same way."[14] Keystone biology has eight units about the cell, including: cell division, energy, homeostasis, DNA, energy maintenance, and ecology. Although the exams are in December and May, it is difficult to cover all material well.

Ironically, the teachers have had to resort to a cyber-class for the ecology unit. It is interesting too that the Keystone exam in biology was instituted the same year the school district distributed iPads to all their students. Each department in the high school implements creative instruction with the iPad, and Craig Whipkey is pleased that: "since we have implemented the iPad technology in the classrooms, our SPP score (school performance profile) has gone up every year." There is value in assessing the way freshman biology students can understand a cell's diverse operations. And it is good too that faculty can provide clear learning goals and objectives that give unambiguous data regarding their teaching effectiveness. Perhaps at the ninth-grade level, learning about the cell in its diverse aspects lays the

---

14. Craig Whipkey in discussion with the author, March 2018. All subsequent quotes from Craig Whipkey are from the March discussion.

groundwork for appreciating life's inherent complexity later in students' intellectual development. But both the standard criteria set by the Keystone exams and the iPad use conspire to foster other concerns, primarily about how students connect parts to wholes and exactly how it is that tactile learning may be confined to digital patterns. When asked about the effects of "teaching to the test" and the use of iPads, Whipkey replies:

> Here is the unfortunate part, when the commonwealth of Pennsylvania moved to the Keystone exam, it was about the same time that we started the iPad initiative; I taught biology prior to that and I can see a noticeable change in retention of information. The students remember and retain where there is a kinesthetic connection of actually writing it down, doing a lab or doing something as an activity that they were able to make a connection. It has changed the method of instruction. Prior to 2010, utilizing notes, worksheets, that went along with reading in the textbooks, required students to read and apply it to a worksheet and handing it in. Now, the reading is on a PDF file, and the worksheet is also a PDF. I can expect to have anywhere from 40–60 percent (of worksheets) copied and circulated among the students. 130 to 170 students have the same exact assignment—and man, it does not take much say, "do you have the biology assignment, and could you send me the assignment?" They split their screen and just copy the answers on to their PDF. It's unbelievable, the level of plagiarism; . . . it requires something else, and we are struggling to find that something else that is doable.

Teaching to the Keystones means there is not time for dissection (as in worms or frogs). But students are learning to dissect and manipulate in very efficient ways the media ecology that can leverage their competitive advantage. The kinesthetic and tactile learning that Craig Whipkey sees as vital to learning has been transposed to the tactile manipulations of screens and data-transfer. Whether students are learning about the "lives of a cell" can be determined somewhat by the state's examinations, but we must acknowledge that a more fundamental pattern of learning is happening implicitly. And this activity looks like data-mining and sharing information to actualize efficiency, nothing more than contemporary business practices. The subtle differences between passing a class with efficient distinction and thinking carefully about abstract relationships (e.g., cells, or numbers for that matter) have become more pronounced. In the words of Whipkey, the freshmen biology class and his elective environmental science class are "two different worlds."

Like Meredith LaFontaine, Whipkey understands the historical and cultural context of learning. He is an avid environmentalist and has become an advocate for sustainability, not only in his county, but in the state and the nation. He has been motivated by the work of Richard Louv and introduced me to Louv's analysis of the *nature deficit disorder*: "The phrase's descriptive quality . . . helps us to get a handle on what children lose without direct contact with the outdoors." Louv states that children who do not encounter nature with openness, "suffer a deficit of health and wonder—an understanding where they fit in the world—and possibly a loss of cognitive acuity."[15] Craig Whipkey has seen many examples of this, the most astounding being that one of his students was sure that if one were to throw corn on a plot of ground, it would automatically grow in rows, as if the configuration of orderly rows in growth were part of corn DNA. His environmental science class has a unit on pollution. He starts that unit by connecting *cause of death* data to students' regional contexts. This is a world apart from "teaching to the test," for it engages juniors and seniors at the existential and affective level. "I open the class with a survey, 'how are you going to die?' The Center for Disease Control has shown that most people die from respiratory illness, cancer, and heart disease. I then show the students data that in Beaver County there is a 40% greater risk of dying from respiratory illness. Why? Because there are five coal-powered plants right here within a thirty-mile radius of the high school. Then I begin the unit on air pollution." Yet Whipkey has received feedback that this critical method can have unintended consequences. Namely, that students become overwhelmed and decide that the future is doomed and their role in sustainability futile. He has gradually changed his pedagogy. Again, this is due to his awareness of the historical moment. He is less concerned with convincing students (and parents) of climate change, but rather, "now, I have to convince students what we can do to help with it."

ENCOUNTER IN FOCUS

Just as Meredith Lafontaine has responded to digital numbness with pedagogies of silence and its significance, Whikpey has responded to students "nature deficit disorder" with an initiative that goes beyond the environmental

15. Shaughnessy, "Features," 4–5.

science curriculum. About ten years ago, Whipkey started the Outdoor Education, Experience, and Exploration Club at the high school in order to "get kids outside, out of the classroom, and out of their normal routine." These outings involve hands-on studies in aquatics, measuring pollutants in freshwater around the county. "Raccoon Creek is frequently shut down because of e-coli levels, they see that a big body of water is heavily impacted by a small trickling stream that would be impacted by run-off or fertilizers." Whipkey is convinced that ecological awareness develops sufficiently through encounters with the intricate relations between infrastructure and water. This kind of encounter is "what students thank us for, . . . the part they always remember." For the past several years, Whipkey's OEEE club has gone to the McKeever Environmental Center in Northwestern Pennsylvania. "They are not allowed phones or iPads at this location." When some of the students heard a woodpecker on this outing, they were frightened: "75 percent of these kids had no clue what the noise of the woodpecker was." What the students thank Craig Whipkey for is showing them how to make their own dinner at the campfire. This is tactile learning at its most fundamental and formidable. To make a fire, cut the vegetables, cooking, and of course eating together, "that part they always remember." The onion that hisses on the fire, its cellular structure burns and cooks, and will be absorbed into the cellular structure of that student who will remember that event. Will the Keystone exam be remembered? Encounters are the crucible for deep learning, learning that forms an intentional consciousness drawn to the full spectacle of human existence. Such intending, as these creative teachers demonstrate, takes persistent work at the edges of normative educational and digital practice. It means largely that they have had to cultivate their own encounters with risk and creativity in order to facilitate a rich process of intellectual integration for their students. Encountering thought in its own ecology of emotion, reason, and meaning demands nothing less. In opening reason beyond its instrumental pattern, we anticipate our own and others' cognitive disruptions. In that process we confirm our memories, and we enter the imagination with a distinct intentionality, one that strengthens its grip on reality as our intentions become more conscious and aware. This awareness integrates an encounter with our own reason, a thinking about thinking, even as it deepens the encounter with an object, person, nature, culture.

2

Openness

An Open Structure Sees the Openings in Structures

DESCRIPTION

FOR MEREDITH LAFONTAINE AND Craig Whipkey, the digital patterns of education had to be both interrupted and opened out to alternative encounters. This is not easy work, for the teachers must adjudicate both their own digital processes and, in their role as leaders of hundreds of students, must persist in cultivating engagements beyond the instrumental routines of culture. Being open to alternative ways, alternative ideas, alternative trajectories is the necessary condition for such interruption. And it is as natural as putting on a coat; except that we might need to think about putting on our coats with our non-dominant arm once in a while; or spend a week walking a different path to the class-room or break room, or figuring the amount of water you use in a day. In these small novel encounters in thought, we come again to the native core of our being, for we are born ready to focus, distinguish, and discover each moment.

OPENNESS AND RELATIONAL STRUCTURE

A human personality learns as a result of a dynamic relational structure. This structure, as it is called by those who study infancy, can become more or less open, depending on its earliest relational patterns. When we are born we share an intrinsic perceptual preference for eyes, face-like patterns, feminine voices. We favor focusing on these dynamic realities. Becoming so focused, we begin to revel in interactions, which become regular channels for our most distinctive human trait: relational awareness. We are born searching for these particular relational moments. A structure is built by these patterns of interactions as relational habits and skills grow moment by moment. We become adept at sharing in these encounters, all the while scaffolding a structure of self-consciousness. Patterns of encounter with parents are indispensable to this process. For example, proto-conversations become delightful interactions whereby "affect imbued action arcs" create patterns. Through these patterns solitariness is diffused through sharing the action, "building it up to a climax before bringing it to conclusion in resolution."[1] The significance of this is that we are born searching. Also, in searching, we simultaneously recognize and participate in relational patterns. We are wired for *discovery*, which has its genesis and end in *encounter*.

TO REPEAT: IT IS KNOWN AS *MIMESIS* IN THE PHILOSOPHICAL TRADITION

Mimicking as a process of solidifying the structures to broaden learning is known in philosophical terminology as *mimesis*. Plato and Aristotle comment on this process in different ways, but both acknowledge its power. As Plato argued in Book 10 of the *Republic*, poetic repetition can serve to make unthinking citizens. In the dialogue with Glaucon, Socrates acknowledges his own love of poetry, especially of Homer, but his concern is about the poet who is nothing more than a "honeyed muse." Conditioned by the "excitement" of poetry, the state will become ruled only by "pleasure and pain," not justice and virtue. For Plato, it is only the refinement of reason that can rise above pleasure and the avoidance of pain. Reason can discern that pleasure and pain-avoidance are often opposed to the interests of those

---

1. Rossmanith and Reddy, "Structure and Openness in the Development of Self in Infancy," 241.

whose primary concern ought to be on virtue and justice.[2] Plato's point is relevant today: through delight, emotions tend to smother more analytic aspects of human reason. Repeating slogans that resonate somehow with one's identity never ensures we have thought deeply about what it is we are saying. On a level of daily routine, it is idiomatic expressions that we repeat in order to either avoid hard analysis or mask ignorance. What really are we saying when we respond to someone's complaint, "*It is what it is. . .*"? Taken to the realm of digitization we can appreciate Plato's concern even more. Children, adolescents, and adults checking their phones persistently is mimetic behavior at rock-bottom. At its worst, mimesis is merely "knee jerk," or actions done at the level of default, or pre-reflectively. If we don't know why we are looking at our devices and do it anyway, we may have become beholden to what Plato was concerned about, empty, un-thinking actions of catharsis. Aristotle certainly understood Plato's concern, but has good things to say about mimesis. Like many of his diagnostic approaches, he takes a broad, comparative view:

> The instinct of imitation is implanted in man from childhood, one difference between him and other animals being that he is the most imitative of living creatures, and through imitation learns his earliest lessons; and no less universal is the pleasure felt in things imitated. We have evidence of this in the facts of experience. Objects which in themselves we view with pain, we delight to contemplate when reproduced with minute fidelity: such as the forms of the most ignoble animals and of dead bodies. The cause of this again is, that to learn gives the liveliest pleasure, not only to philosophers but to men in general; whose capacity, however, of learning is more limited.[3]

Yes, Aristotle, it is fun to imitate animals! I have a friend named Ben. He is now a lawyer, but was for many years an actor. He claimed he got some of his humor from his grandfather who, when Ben and his grandmother would come home from the store, would be sitting in his chair, pretending to be dead. I'll leave it to you to decide if this is funny. At any rate, Aristotle's point is important, for we do delight in imitation and therefore we do delight at this level of learning. But repetition of animal behavior or becoming corpse-like is one thing, posting images mimetically is another, and constantly checking our devices is, as I said, quite another. Let

2. Plato, *The Republic*, 330–32.
3. Aristotle, *Poetics*, 6–7.

us see how, at the stage of infancy, we delight in learning, but importantly, become open to difference and novelty in the patterns of encounter, thus forming an intellect of openness. The relational structure that is built for discovery has three significant dimensions that lead us to openness. These are anticipation, co-regulation of inter-actions, and variability. When variability becomes a part of the movement toward discovery the *openness* of this structure can see the *openings* in patterns and structures. With the aid of phenomenological psychologists Rossmanith and Reddy, we can trace the mimetic proto-conversation as a proto-encounter, which will give us insight into the necessity and nature of intellectual openness.

ANTICIPATION

If a seven-month old has experienced consistently the inter-action loops of a proto-conversation, she begins to anticipate them. Ironically enough, there must be a pre-linguistic form of "if this, then that," the schematic substrate of her anticipation. It seems to me that this is logical thinking at its most basic, its fundamental junction: sequence. The sequence is the pattern perceived by both parent and child. A previous encounter is remembered and recollected, drawing out the emotive line of reasoning called anticipation. Perception, memory, and anticipation facilitate what phenomenologists describe as the "displacement of the self."[4] Losing oneself one gains a self. The native intelligence that conditions our being displaced, strengthens our very sense of place, our being in the world. Here, the native power in the distinct moments of perception, memory, and imagination structure open intelligence. Anticipation of encounter involves a series of sequential possibilities. Anticipation of encounter demonstrates reflexivity, the very vital sense that we become aware of others' awareness of us. The pattern of the proto-conversation is impossible without this reflexive awareness. Once the pattern has yielded reflexivity it seems to me that awareness is intransigent. Though it may be dulled or numbed by neglect, or saturated with undue attention, self-conscious reflexivity is the developing personality's structural foundation that can be built by an infinite array of subsequent relational encounters. Despite the seemingly infinite possibility of ongoing encounters, our point is that we anticipate them as relational learning processes, and this anticipation can become frozen (reified) in adolescence and adulthood. Robert Sokolowski has said:

4. Sokolowski, *Introduction to Phenomenology*, 74.

We may take such projections of the self for granted and assume that anyone can easily perform them, but in some situations it takes considerable ego strength to be able to carry them out effectively. For some people at some times the strain of realistically imagining themselves into new circumstances is too great; they collapse emotionally and get all confused, and their self does not have the flexibility plus the identity to project into circumstances they have not lived through.[5]

If there is only inflexible routine, predictable schema, ubiquity of digital encounter, the energy of the personality's anticipatory structure can become inert. This we might call a static predisposition to encounter and it may curtail the mind's broader potentialities. This may be the case especially if we have not become proficient in patterns of relation that foster the two other dimensions of openness, co-regulative and variable learning in encounter.

CO-REGULATORS: THE WE FACTOR

In a proto-conversation, at one point the infant may initiate the interaction. Perhaps mimicking mother or father's cadence and sticking out the tongue as they do. In that initiation of the pattern, both parent and infant become conscious of the normative or regular aspects of the encounter; a *familiar* cadence intoned within the family's relational world. A deeper awareness is then instantiated, the self-conscious awareness that the infant is part of a larger whole. Recognizing a shared norm of rhythm with voice and tongue, the infant becomes a co-creator of the pattern, aware of this power. Self-conscious direction of the pattern means that we become conscious of our part in the whole of the process. Becoming partially responsible for the pattern, co-regulation is the fundamental principle of integration and we begin to become focused on seeing connected parts relative to larger wholes. As phenomenological study would articulate it, consciousness is always *consciousness of* something. Awareness is always intentional awareness. Co-regulatory patterns demonstrate the fluidity of the self in perception. In other words, our preoccupation with a singular selfhood is something of a delusion. An unadulterated self, free from the constraining airs that burden my capacity to be me, seems not to correspond to this early phenomenological interpretation. We are intellectually formed first by a search

5. Sokolowski, *Introduction to Phenomenology*, 73.

and participation in a *we*. The mind is a public thing.[6] Only secondarily do we learn to search "me." Encounter is a fundament of learning routines. We build the structure of our personality from the we, from parental intimacy to familial structure, from community to nation.

VARIABILITY

Now that the proto-conversation has been firmly established into its pattern, and the infant has become conscious of his or her co-regulative capacities, we can see that encounters are not only based on previous ones, but that more complex co-regulative processes will supersede patterns that no longer stimulate participants. Novelty is brought forth through relational variability. Rossmanith and Reddy provide an example:

> Around the middle of the first year infants play a much more obvious role in setting up new interactive structures and violating structures that they have just mastered or accepted. . . . Such clowning might involve shaking the head repeatedly, making funny sounds, odd facial expressions. . . . In teasing, infants use structure (as do adults in even more complex ways) to take the relationship further; the violations cause surprise, alarm, amusement, and then a denouement, a coming together into a deeper level of resolution and intimacy.[7]

Infant experiments; is that not what our researchers describe? We are born scientists of encounter, testing and creating beyond the established convention, the norm as it has been implicitly agreed upon. Testing as they do, infants also interrupt the patterns set by mimetic practice; they play with them and transpose their previous meaning, seeking a deeper encounter, a novel patterning. The established structure of the learning personality is invariable: anticipation—co-regulation—variability. But that singular dimension of variability means the structure coheres by a capacity to imagine and facilitate novel relational patterns. Think about the multidimensional richness of a simple mimetic encounter: attuned to the capacity to vary patterns, infancy structures human creativity by leveraging perception, memory, and imagination for the purpose of deeper knowing. This is the germ of successive intellectual openness. Such openness grows out of encounters. Openness involves the expectation that in co-regulating

6. Sokolowski, *Introduction to Phenomenology*, 11–12.

7. Rossmanith, "Structure and Openness," 245.

patterns of relational knowledge we can stretch or change those patterns. The openness of structure sees the openings in structures.

BINDING STRUCTURE: BOUND TO FREEDOM OF THOUGHT

What binds the structure of personality together is this fluid coherence of anticipation, regulation, and variability. We are capable of degrees of variability by which we test and deepen our encounters with others, leading to an adept analysis of patterns and their renewal or even dismissal. These encounters through which we test (and are tested); bind us first to our remembering and secondly to our anticipatory imaginations. The first move toward openness is an interrogation of the perceptions of encounter, imagined with multi-faceted ideas and possible eventualities. Also, since the foundation of searching is relational through and through, we are bound to others, absorbing and appreciating conditional knowledge of previous encounters, and with that focus, proposing possible actualities of foresight which would strengthen the pattern of connection. Bound to these rich data, we can then configure variables, which would renew the pattern or change the pattern to the extent that we induce a novel undergoing. Hewn out of encounters, an openness and freedom in thought first must be practiced in the established structures of experience. As we are bound to those patterns, as we are bound to others, so we are bound to our intelligence which would build from the structure a varied edifice for knowing. The times tables are necessary for quadratic equations; the minor and major scales are necessary for jazz improvisation; grammatical rules are necessary for creative prose and poetry. As we are bound to structure, so we are free to play, explore, and extend pattern and structure. But two things are necessary for the open-ended play to commence. We must not only know, but appreciate, the *regula* (rule/pattern). And we need to encounter in others consistent variation in fostering and changing patterns. This is why proto-conversation is such a lucid example of the move toward intellectual openness; its form is the same from babble to bi-lateral diplomacy. At its best, conversation refines intuitions, affirms deductions, enriches powers of description, disposes one to hospitality, redacts and sifts truth. Conversation makes one responsible, and creatively so.

OPENNESS AS RESPONSIVENESS

Mid-twentieth-century Yale Divinity School professor H. Richard Niebuhr's (1894–1962) moral ideas seem a scaled premonition of Rossmanith's and Reddy's findings. I say "scaled" because in Niebuhr's thought, what I call the infancy experiments yielding openness become a capability of moral reflection in adulthood. Responsibility involves its refined capacity for searching, regulating, and variation. Niebuhr's final reflections, found on his desk at the time of his death, were prepared for lectureships in Scotland, the University of Glasgow, and California, Pacific School of Religion. According to both his son Richard R. Niebuhr and his celebrated student James Gustafson, they represent thirty years of teaching, dialogue, and thinking about moral life in conversation with philosophy, the social sciences, and the church. Though the preface acknowledges the dislike some may have for such a designation, H. Richard Niebuhr's writing is called "Christian moral philosophy." Not unlike the phenomenology of infancy described above, these particular reflections of Niebuhr's possess a tripartite structure, a way to think through openness and responsiveness that intimates a dynamic between routine and the co-regulation of novelty.

Niebuhr's posthumously published *The Responsible Self* argued that human beings are goal setters and law followers, but primarily, and most significantly, responders. Influenced by Martin Buber's seminal existential philosophy of the human person, Niebuhr placed encounter at the center of his moral proposal. First, however, he examined the two most influential ethical frameworks of his day, those of Aristotle (384–322 BCE) and Immanuel Kant (1724–1804). From these philosophical giants he suggested that human beings have a purpose (Aristotle) and need good laws (Kant). Having a purpose means we develop goals for ourselves and make our way toward those goals, becoming agents of development. Following laws conduces us to recognize order and appreciate laws that are true and good. It is also important to be able, with Kant, to know bad laws from good, a discussion in *The Responsible Self* that reveals Niebuhr's concern with the events of the twentieth-century civil rights movement and the evil of segregation.

Though Niebuhr acknowledges these indispensable moments in moral development, he proposes that human beings are faced with much more complex realities that reason must encounter squarely if it is to develop a sanative life. Niebuhr suggests that in many ways life happens to us. We are beholden to unbidden voices, experiences, and events. "We interpret the things that force themselves upon us as parts of wholes . . . and these large patterns of interpretation we employ seem to determine—though in no mechanical way—our responses to action upon us."[8] Therefore, our intelligence is led to ask a question, "What is going on?" Having come to some tentative, if reasonable conclusion about that question, then Niebuhr says that the focus of our moral energies should be: *In light of my tentative answer to what is going on, what is the proper response?*[9] Both, what is going on? and, what is the proper response? must take into account ultimate goals (like loving and being loved) and established norms and laws (like a pattern for relations). But those questions precede all others. We encounter and interpret the moral context, we do not invent it.

Ultimately, these questions configure reason as bending toward responsiveness: to the patterns we interpret, to the imagination, to others, and to our own creative freedom. Notice how general are Niebuhr's questions. Their form is that of inquiry, of course, and open searching, and they provide general dispositions by which we might approach particular contexts. If we align Niebuhr's categories with the infant's structural awareness, we see analogous, if not symmetrical categories.

Encountering Moral Complexities	Infant Encounter
Goal setters	Anticipation
Law followers	Co-regulators
Responsive	Open variation

Like variation, responsibility takes some semblance of autonomy and risk. Responding is an ability that is implicitly open because the questions prior to response are so general. As such they become applicable to the details and specifics of particular contexts. For example, for Meredith La-Fontaine, what is going on with high-school student stress has something to do with the digitization of their lives, hence the proper response, formal quiet. For Albert Borgmann, his theory applied to historical fact concludes that the food-production pattern resulted in the public-health concern of obesity. This leads to the capacity to ask a responsible question: Given that historical development, what are some ways to think about the proper responses to the hyper-production of information and its attendant devices?

Niebuhr's moral phenomenology places onto communities and regions the task of figuring the economic and ecologic context of a place,

8. Niebuhr, *The Responsible Self*, 61–62.
9. Niebuhr, *The Responsible Self*, 65–67.

and then, being open to proposing novel patterns in order to pursue the good. Digital, convenient, consumptive patterns and presumptions block reason's innate search for variability. They are the default, mimetic process of reason at the national and commercial levels. They are the intransigent principles driving consumption, the individualist goals driving political rhetorics of fear. We must interrupt bottom-line and efficiency thinking to forge a region's public questions. What is going in here with water, refuse, transportation, gentrification, access to education and nature? Without probing questions, which suspend ready-made assumptions, we are left to the devices of market and monolith, of convenience and commercialization, and some of us live, under our protective shells, in illusion.

OPENNESS AND FORESIGHT

The open disposition is a searching disposition. Minding the search, we ask the questions that are themselves responses, responses to evidential matters that provide more grist for the mill of the inquiring mind. As the infant tests—if this, then that—so does the open personality, cognizant of the complex interrelationship between goals, rules, and freedom, and fundamentally aware of the goals, order, and creativity of the human mind. The open person knows there is probably more to understand, but trusts that, given her findings thus far, she can allow her openness to see more clearly probable openings looming on the horizon. This is what Alfred North Whitehead has called foresight. Another triad, Whitehead's foresight has three related dimensions: stability, understanding, and a discerning judgment of facts from which a vision of the future may emerge. Foresight can only come from a pre-existing routine, structure, and pattern. Whitehead explores the meaning of foresight in his *Adventures of Ideas*, a learned consideration of the slow development of social, scientific, and philosophical theories' historical embodiments. His own foresight seems to be expressed here; he could well be discussing the development of the internet and the digital mimesis described above, when in 1933 he wrote: "A system will be the product of intelligence. But when the adequate routine is established, intelligence vanishes, and the system is maintained by a coordination of conditioned reflexes."[10] His point is that civilization needs routine-bearers, those who cultivate the stability of patterns or systems so that people may live securely and together. But civilizations that focus solely on the

10. Whitehead, *Adventures of Ideas*, 114.

maintenance and systems of routine become little more than colonies of ants. Foresight demands understanding, which, according to Whitehead, is "a philosophic power of understanding the complex flux of the varieties of human societies: for instance, the habit of noting varieties of demands on life, of serious purposes, of frivolous amusements."[11]

This understanding ought to become a habit if one is going to offer some lasting insight for a probable condition of future existence. The third aspect Whitehead thinks important in foresight is the ability to cull the relevant facts from which the future is to emerge. In short, "foresight is the product of insight."[12] As Craig Whipkey said, he has moved from convincing his students that climate change is happening, to inviting them to consider how they might live in order to restore ecological vitality. He has based this speculative process on regional truths and concrete encounters. Forecasts are mimetically generated; foresight derives from encounters of understanding.

Nicole Rossmanith and Vasudevi Reddy, H. Richard Niebuhr and Alfred North Whitehead; all affirm intellectual openness. Openness to others, ideas, nature, the future, depends upon the dynamic relation between pattern and variability. An open intelligence must learn, understand, and appreciate pre-ordained patterns while simultaneously inserting or spotting openings in those same patterns. The more one is opened up to variability in patterns and patterning, the more one can begin to connect patterns, one to the next. This work takes encounter seriously, since, in order to be able to sift the intellectual germinations of these experiences, we search out new encounters to test and nourish them. Openness as an encounter of thought is risky because we may come up against our most cherished ideas, patterns of thinking that may have become brittle. It is helpful to look to minds who have trodden the ground before us. Albert Borgmann has said of Thomas Merton that he had an "intrepid openness."[13] In our encounter with this Trappist monk from Kentucky, we see an exemplification not only of one who had powerfully deep encounters with others and with nature, but one who learned very early in life to come into these encounters with an integrated openness, an openness born of the synergy of head and heart.

11. Whitehead, *Adventures of Ideas*, 123.

12. Whitehead, *Adventures of Ideas*, 113.

13. For an extended reflection on Borgmann's interpretation of Merton's prophetic openness, see my "Borgmann on Merton: Exploring the Possibility of Contemplation in a Technological Age."

OPENNESS EXEMPLIFIED: THOMAS MERTON

In 1939, two years before he would become a Trappist monk, and one year after he was received into the Catholic Church, Thomas Merton was alone in his apartment in Greenwich Village, "sitting cross-legged on the floor like Gandhi."[14] There he was reading and meditating on Scripture, a mode of openness through which "engaged readers are . . . enabled to discover otherwise inaccessible dimensions of their deepest selves." Merton was involved in a "do-it-yourself retreat using the Spiritual Exercises of Saint Ignatius."[15] The Ignatian Spiritual Exercises invite a meditative journey into such horrid biblical scenes as the slaughter of the innocents, drawing readers to a "vivid imaginative engagement with the Scriptures, involving in this process the whole person, the so-called three powers of the soul, memory, intellect and will."[16] Merton would not stop with these exercises in meditation; he would press on in response, transposing the scenes he had observed through his imagination into poetry. The meditation on the slaughter of the innocents, based on Matthew 2:13–18, expands out to the escape from terror: Mary, Joseph, and Jesus, being spared by their exile in Egypt. Now a conduit, Merton would transpose these scenes in a contemporary idiom evoking a deeper awareness of both place and time: urban tenements, Hitler's slaughtering.[17] Merton opened himself. To the Exercises, which invite imaginative participation in the scene, to the scene itself by placing himself in the scene, and to the suffering world, constantly barraged by evil. All this led to the depth of poetic insight. The structure of Ignatian and other "spiritual exercises" are invitations to participate in the synergy between pattern and variability. It's an invitation we enter, as it were, at our own risk.

There are many of his generation who were attuned deeply to modernity's violent and turgid crescendo, but few were as articulate, and fewer still were as comprehensive in their scope of analysis and response as Thomas Merton, Trappist monk, writer, poet. I will name some of the conversations he moved forward, shaped, and continues to influence.

---

14. O'Connell, "From *Lectio* to Lyric," 311–45, 314–15.

15. O'Connell, "From *Lectio* to Lyric," 312, 314.

16. O'Connell, "From *Lectio* to Lyric," 314.

17. O'Connell, "From *Lectio* to Lyric," 316.

- The problem of white racism
- The promise and perils of Marxism
- poetry and literary criticism in general
- ecological consciousness/crisis
- ecclesial and monastic reform
- philosophy of technology
- inter-religious dialogue and pacificism

All of this was pursued in addition to, or grew directly as a result of, his seminal understanding of the ancient Christian contemplative tradition and its tremendous impact on language, literature, and meaning in Western consciousness. This appreciation of diverse Christian traditions of spirituality was in part due to his responsibility as the master (teacher) of novices at the Monastery, Gethsemane: where he lived for half of his life. One must possess and cultivate an intrepid openness in order to penetrate confidently and intelligently all of these topics. Let's be clear, Merton was not just interested in these matters as some sort of hobby of intelligence; no, he understood them pastorally, in their significance as a sign of human plenitude, and he could articulate clearly and simply that significance. In some sense, Merton must have been able to see how they were all connected. And, working the angles of those connections; conveyed penetrating insight into each part, so that his audience/readers might draw closer to their own capacity for openness, attention, and awareness. This kind of openness, attention, and awareness can also lead us into risky territory. I once interviewed a priest on the anniversary of his ordination, which happened to be the anniversary of the start of Vatican II. I was asking about pastoral love and the capacity of a priest to become open to others in their ministry. He said, "I don't think a man would be a good priest if he could not fall in love."[18] The implication is that being open and responding out of love to the needs and presence of others cannot be actualized without the beautiful human tendency to be opened up; opened for the kind of intimacy necessary to care in a mutual encounter authentically.

In 1966, Merton's openness resulted in his falling in love with a nurse at the Louisville Hospital where he was having back surgery—her name

18. Msgr. William Biebel (1936–2016), Interviews by Aaron K. Kerr, June 9, 16, 30, August 25, September 9, 2011. Transcript. It will be housed at the Personal Archive, Erie, PA.

was Margie. The romance was never consummated, but he was captivated with the relationship. It seemed mostly to be mutual delight in conversation. From 1960 on he was reading carefully the journals and writings of Kierkegaard, Jacques and Raissa Maritain (a French married couple who impacted Merton greatly), and Albert Camus, among others. Open to the authentic intellectual and spiritual struggles of those he admired, he made sense of his brief but powerful relationship with Margie, and his resolution to cut it off and remain a committed monk. By way of an open reading of others' personal struggles, especially Camus' notion of absurdity, he was able to work out the meaning of his monastic commitment. Specifically, listening carefully to the atheist Camus, but ultimately disagreeing with Camus' vision, he broke off the romantic relationship.[19] He was also open to American culture. He appreciated the literary movement known as the Beats, particularly Jack Kerouac and Lawrence Ferlinghetti, those who influenced the likes of the Grateful Dead. He was intrigued with Bob Dylan; he met with pacifist singer and songwriter Joan Baez and dedicated an essay on pacifism to her. At the same time, he was corresponding with young feminist theologian Rosemary Radford Ruether, met with a Sufi (Islamic) mystic, and a much younger Dalai Lama. Being genuine encounters, these persons impacted his writing and vocation in special ways. His deep knowledge and incisive writing comes out of relational knowing.

19. There are interesting interpretations of this relationship. And since openness to loving both others and ideas are in a pretty complex dynamic energy, we need to attune to the way desire functions in our learning. As the classical tradition, notably Plato, has made clear, the erotic is inter-fused with the rational desire for intelligibility and consistency. And as Merton was deeply immersed in the Christian contemplative tradition of love, perhaps starting with the Song of Songs, we need to take those contexts seriously in interpreting this openness to romance. I believe the complex is flattened out by certain contemporary, I would say, "therapeutic" and individualist interpretations of these events. My point, it is primarily *because of* the intense pattern of contemplation, poetry, and prayer, that Merton could have been open to Margie and those same resources led to his cutting it off. Robert Hudson, in *The Monk's Record Player*, aligns Merton's discontent with monastic life with both his falling in love and his interest in Bob Dylan, using the language of independence, and to my mind projecting this modernist fallacy onto Merton. A more realistic interpretation is that of Ramon Cao Martinez, who suggests that Merton's thinking and writing at the same time the romance was building led to the rejection of Camus' absurdist ethics of quantity, "the will to multiply the number and the variety of life experiences." Disagreeing with Camus' ethic, Martinez suggests, affirmed his relinquishment of this romance, bound as he was to the singular experience of a Monk's life. See Hudson, *The Monk's Record Player*, 65–150 and Martinez "The Readings of a Diarist," 347–51.

Our minds, saturated as they are with the cult of celebrity, need to interrupt that sometimes-superficial glance of the *cause celebre* and remember that Merton was a monk, who struggled piously (in the best sense of that word) with speaking out against the war,[20] and he also struggled with his love for the young nurse. Obedience to the religious pattern was essential to his identity. He understood that in the complex of his soul, some of what he was struggling with was his ego, just as he understood his earlier struggles with wanting to become a Carthusian or becoming a hermit, a struggle with sin. In that way, he is just like us. But, his awareness and depth of understanding the manifold dimensions of a variety of topics is exemplary and seems particularly graced. Our appreciation of the structure of openness as being able to see the opening in structures certainly can be illuminated by considering the dynamic relation between patterns and variability in the life of a monk. Above I suggested that an open intelligence must not only know by rote, but also learn to *appreciate* through participation in the pattern before it. Indeed, as the infant learns to appreciate the pattern, they must live within it; only then can they creatively engage and open the pattern in novel ways. Here is the pattern of the monk's life at the Trappist monastery in Kentucky, in the decade of the 1940s; the place of Merton's intrepid openness.[21]

2:00 a.m. Sung Prayer	11:30 a.m. Dinner
2:30 a.m. Meditation	12:15 p.m. Reading/prayer
3:00 a.m. Night Office: Scriptural/psalmody	1:30 p.m. Work
4:00 a.m. Private Masses/others receive, private prayer	3:30 p.m. Reading/private prayer
5:30 a.m. First Daylight Prayer/breakfast	4:30 p.m. Evening Prayer
6:30 a.m. Reading/study	5:15 p.m. Meditation
7:45 a.m. Mass (readings/homily/Eucharist)	5:30 p.m. A light refreshment
9:00 a.m. Work	6:10 p.m. Prayers
10:45 a.m. Reading/private prayer	7:00 p.m. All retire
11:07 a.m. Praying Psalms	

Can we imagine living so methodically and simply? Perhaps we see constraint and the fetters of terse time? But let's take a closer look. Out of a

20. Merton, *Passion for Peace*, 27.

21. Merton, *Entering the Silence*, 489. I have taken liberty with the language, making it more descriptive of the activity undertaken, less Latinate and "religious."

seventeen-hour day, if we take meditation time and reading times together, a monk could spend four hours and forty-five minutes in thought, meditation, and reading a day. Solitude. And if, like Merton, one "entered the silence" with anticipation, imagination, a searching heart and mind, basically with deep intentionality, this pattern would begin to see many openings, not only in one's own mind and heart, but in the dynamics of history, the variability in translations and hearings of Scripture, the constancy of a creative grasp of all one encountered. And of course, all these encounters might be infused, at certain times, with an awareness of the very Source of the mind, heart, Scripture, and history.

Now, I am certainly not suggesting, as if caught in nostalgia, that we need to renew education in this ancient pattern. I hope the larger point is clear; namely, that those of us that teach and those of us that learn are often constrained by patterns that keep us locked into routines of technical narrowness, not the aspiration of openness for free thought that colleges and universities claim is their inheritance. What the monk's solitude and Merton's intrepid openness and depth can teach is to ask the following questions: Why do we live without the life-giving power of solitude? What is keeping us from solitude? Why might we scoff or become enmeshed in our busy-ness when we are confronted with the idea, articulated by Meredith LaFontaine: "There goes theology doing nothing again."? Of course, thinking is always happening on various levels as long as we draw breath. But inner solitude is the beginning of a deeper awareness. The exact opposite of "doing nothing" occurs in solitude: the dynamism of thought thinking about itself. This becomes the catalyst for inner and outer transformation.

Learning solitude is a prerequisite to any openness. On the level of infancy it is the "displacement of the self" through imagination and memory. In the classroom it is the displacement of all of the following: my pet ideas, what the teacher wants, what my friends think of me, what the right answer for the exam is. And where is reason displaced to? That's just it, new places. If you like neuroscientific accounts: solitude is the catalyst for growing dendrites and the firing of new synapses. Solitude is *the* good of all learning. In the instrumental and economic terms so pronounced in higher education today, solitude is a "silent partner" in learning. Solitude is a hidden asset, an asset for learning that we forget about and even avoid. What does it mean that higher education has turned its back on this powerful tool for thinking? It is free. You only have to count the cost of unplugging. It just takes the hard work of entering it ourselves; and, knowing how to invite others to enter into it. When we understand the great intellectual power of solitude, we interrogate it as a moral good. It is a good that needs to be opened again in the current digital pattern, in order that we might become ever opened to truth. Solitude is the moral norm of any good education, as it is the *fundament* of the search for truth. Is not the phrase "the search for truth" on every branded liberal arts college in the United States? And what do we encounter in solitude? We can learn from Merton the kind of good it is, but it is a good, alas, that most of us do not want. The asset of solitude measures us, and when we are open, that openness has another side: emptiness. This is a truth about human beings, and Merton helps us to understand that truth's power.

In an essay called "Notes for a Philosophy of Solitude," Merton acknowledges two aspects of human existence that are good in their functional structure. First, those who make a pretense to solitude as some sort of self-righteous independence from others are living "an individualistic illusion." Society is good, as in Whitehead's bearers of routine or Niebuhr's law-abiding citizens. And in society self-transcendence and becoming a person are contingent upon "service to others." But both of these can devolve into what Merton calls *diversion*; the first sub-heading of this 1960 essay is "The Tyranny of Diversion." Merton seems to anticipate Borgmann's more fully articulated device paradigm (1984) by saying that diversion is "systematic distraction," and can be described as: "Those occupations and recreations, so mercifully provided by society, which enable a man to avoid his own company for twenty-four hours a day."[22] He articulates well the depressive under-belly of the technological pattern; it involves: "The anguish of realizing that underneath the apparently logical pattern of a more or less 'well organized' and rational life, there lies an abyss of irrationality, confusion, pointlessness, and indeed of apparent chaos."[23] And yet, Merton asserts the truth that "every man is a solitary, held firmly by the inexorable limitations of his own aloneness."[24] Why? Because we all undergo death alone. This is the paradox the essay illuminates, that we are all together in that singular experience of our loneliness. This emptiness awaits us on the other side of our openness. And this is why digital diversion is so tempting. But let us explore this emptiness in terms of its educative promise. For

---

22. Merton, *Selected Essays*, 66. Using a Borgmann term, solitude would be the prevenient *focal practice* necessary for openness to other focal practices.

23. Merton, *Selected Essays*, 67.

24. Merton, *Selected Essays*, 68.

Merton, the emptiness is marked by an awareness that perhaps, some of my aspirations and amusements are absurd and meaningless. Therefore, solitude leads to questions, the perennial questions covered in any good liberal arts curricula: Who am I? What is evil? Is there a God? Did my mother really love me? What is good? How shall I live my life? In asking these questions we realize how difficult life is. And, as Merton holds open the door to our emptiness, in an informed solitude the student "accepts the difficulty of facing the million things in his life which are incomprehensible, instead of simply ignoring them."[25] This encounter with our own emptiness is also the encounter with the existential weight and urgency of our capacity for honest inquiry. Which is why, ultimately, this emptiness will be both "destiny and joy." Why? Well, if we trust the words of the monk:

> But the emptiness is for the sake of fullness: the purpose of the solitary life is, if you like, contemplation. But not contemplation in the pagan sense of an intellectual, esoteric enlightenment achieved by ascetic technique. The contemplation of the Christian solitary is the awareness of the divine mercy transforming and elevating his own emptiness and turning it into the presence of perfect love, perfect fullness.[26]

Sounds like good news to me. But think about how the monk's engagement in routine and pattern led to this conclusion. It was a pattern in solitude and encounter. In solitude, we encounter our own emptiness. In communal engagements, say worship, we encounter others and the Other. In a 2003 essay called "Interiorizing Monasticism," Lawrence Cunningham conveys Merton's monastic openness as "a purveyor of certain values and insights to the larger world of religious seekers."[27] In other words, the work of solitude and inquiry are everyone's task. Cunningham points to Merton's summation and tangible implications of intentional and informed solitude in an address he gave on October 23, 1968, just weeks before his death by accidental electrocution on December 10, 1968. In the notes prepared for that address, Merton describes three gifts monastic life preserves and offers to the larger world.

25. Merton, *Selected Essays*, 67.

26. Merton, *Selected Essays*, 74–75.

27. O'Connell, ed. *The Vision of Thomas Merton*, 65–75, 66.

1. A certain detachment from ordinary concerns for life, a solitude of varying intensity and duration.

2. A preoccupation with the radical inner depths of one's religious and philosophical beliefs, the grounds of those beliefs and their spiritual implications.

3. A particular concern with inner transformation and the deepening of consciousness of a transcendent dimension of life beyond the empirical self.[28]

Another triad:

a) An interruption.

b) An encounter with memory, imagination, analysis, and anticipation.

c) A desire for a newness, a transformative deepening intimacy whose end is beyond the ego.

Think of the first-year college student who is told she or he is to become a "critical" thinker—not a thinker, mind you, a *"critical"* thinker. What does that even mean? It has meant, largely, someone full of cynicism and doubt. But let us intentionally water down Merton's general process of monastic solitude; and see what it takes to invite an intellectual openness today:

a) *Detachment from ordinary concerns for life*: The open learner should develop the habit of abstraction, an abstraction that demands that one suspend the values that captivate one's mind, in order to carefully consider and perhaps even adopt the ideas and free thoughts of those who have traversed the human landscape before us.

b) *A preoccupation with one's religious and philosophical beliefs*: Open learners take time to interrogate their own beliefs, to develop rational justifications for how to understand both themselves and the world around them.

c) *The deepening of consciousness of a transcendent dimension*: An open encounter with your reason will be a life-long pursuit, an ability to find meaning and purpose beyond materials aims.

28. O'Connell, ed. *The Vision of Thomas Merton*, 70; see also, Merton, *The Asian Journal*, 309–10.

In order to instantiate the pattern of solitude in our educational pursuits, perhaps we ought to look to a practice that evokes both solitary and social encounters simultaneously. It is a practice that also grips the encounter with openness as the dynamic relation between pattern and variability. This is reading. Openness to self and others is made possible through the practice of reading. This practice, in its multi-dimensionality, in its informational and knowledge-bearing aspect, in its focal rendering of understanding, can enhance greatly the process of becoming capable human beings.

OPENNESS APPLIED: READING

"The Rabbi of Berditchev saw a man hurrying along the street, looking neither right nor left. 'Why are you rushing so?' he asked him. 'I am after my livelihood,' the man replied.

'And how do you know,' continued the rabbi, 'that your livelihood is running on before you, so that you have to rush after it? Perhaps it is behind you, and all you need to do to encounter it is to stand still—but you are running away from it!'"

—MARTIN BUBER

Reading takes time, as do many focal practices that enrich us. Reading calls one to solitude. When reading a great novel, for example, we may not want it to end, but that certainly does not keep us from stealing time in anticipation of how things might turn out. Such enjoyment is evidence of the way rational engagement has aspects that are indifferent toward efficient aims. Even if you "just want to finish this book," it is not usually due to being able to check it off your to-do list, or add one more book to that numeric list, "Books I Have Read." It is because you want to think it through, be somewhat introspective or gain a deeper appreciation of your place in time. The book is also a medium. Like digital media, it takes up its position between us and reality. But there are considerable differences between reading a book and being online or searching one's phone. The most obvious one involves the nature of embodiment. The studious body is figured differently than the digital body, usually. The body scanning is figured differently than the body turning pages pensively. But the kind of reading that I sometimes see students doing in the library is most distinctive in its sense of time; it is taking time with the book. This ancient practice is a most active mental process. Something is happening, but it is not merely hustling activity to become successful. Nor is it merely finding information, though that is certainly a part of the whole process. Contemporary reading has a particular context that may tell us something about the nature of our culture. When we interrupt the habits established by commercial culture, we can become opened to alternative practices and inevitably to alternative ideas.

HYPER-REALITY: THE DIGITAL TRANSPOSITION OF READING

Reading has long been analogously related to consumption. The Hebrew prophets attest well to their call to "eat the scroll of truth" and then prophesy to a broken world. In that tradition, ideas and truth are consumed through the book, even as the prophet is consumed with zeal for the sacred truth of God.[29] Today, the technocratic-economic system, another way of saying digital culture, has revitalized reading. Reading has been transposed. Speaking most generally, since the 1996 telecommunications act, an internet gold rush has transformed media; many companies have blossomed only to be gobbled up by established corporate entities. Every prospect of digital reading is accompanied by commercialization; there is just no way around it. We are perpetually distracted readers. The machinations that produce what is set before our reading eyes want our loyal attention. In the '60s, Merton saw this as a matter of a reader's intentionality. Reading is a good habit. But it can become a dead letter if not interrupted by our own intentional awareness. Habitual scanning can blunt our attention, closing us off rather than opening us up.

> Nine tenths of the news, as printed in the papers, is pseudo news, manufactured events. Some days ten-tenths. The ritual morning trance, in which one scans columns of news-print, creates a peculiar form of generalized pseudo-attention to a pseudo-reality.[30]

With what foresight does Merton see our current culture! He could be on the reading list and justify the perceptions of both the anti-propagandistic

29. Ezek 2:8—3:3.
30. Merton, *Faith and Violence*, 151.

radical left, like philosopher Noam Chomsky, as well as the fire-brand former White House chief strategist, the populist Steve Bannon. What Merton insightfully articulated as the "ritual morning trance" reveals that the displacement of our attention by *manufactured* events is not new, it has just become spasmodic and hyper. In her *Slow Philosophy*, Michelle Boulous Walker summarizes the effects of digital culture on our reading habits. Online reading develops "skimming techniques." These techniques are not bad in themselves, but Walker points out that they "are finding their way back to our complex everyday reading encounters, with the result that our reading abilities are impaired." Findings in neuroscience affirm this transposition, making newly established circuits compete with "deep reading circuitry." Also, online reading has a different spatiality; it is "non-linear" reading. Basically, in order to surmount or shortcut all the extraneous distractions of pop-ups, pictures, and hyper-links our reading is reduced to quick scanning, searching for key words.[31] Walker makes it clear that digital media transpose reading, refining reason's metrical analysis, a honing mechanism for pattern or digits, letters and words. This kind of reading is good only if it is accompanied by times of deeper analysis in encounter. An over-amplified metrical reading tends to make readers hyper-consumers of data, the context is left out of that equation. Metrical reading also strengthens the illusion that winning information efficiently is the same as understanding something sufficiently. Efficient reading is not sufficient reading. Put baldly, possessing information gives one no sense of what to do with it or how it might connect to other aspects of information culled elsewhere. Nor does efficiently won information necessarily evoke the imaginative capacities necessary for holistic perception. A sufficient reading, of both text and context, must have something that is not in any way a part of the current definition of efficiency, namely, resting in time, resisting hyper-activity or activity aimed solely at efficiency. With Buber's Rabbi of Bertichev, how do we know that the truth of our lives is ahead of us? Maybe it is behind us, trying to catch up, and we must be still in order that we might encounter the truth of our very livelihood. Reading and reading slowly are habits that can open us to this existential truth of our inward being. It seems a matter of approach. Let us slow down and focus on a focal practice. I invite you to read Albert Borgmann's reflection on the approach one takes to a family meal contrasted with the consumption that has resulted from what in 1984

---

31. Walker, *Slow Philosophy*, 13.

he called the "food industry." In the quote below, try, as I have, to substitute *information* for food and *reading* for eating/meal, take your time.

> Once food has become freely available, it is only consistent that the gathering of the meal is shattered and disintegrates into snacks, T.V. dinners, bites that are grabbed to be eaten; and eating itself is scattered around television shows, late and early meetings, activities, overtime work, and other business. This is increasingly, the normal condition of technological eating. But it is within our power to clear a central space amid the clutter and distraction. We can begin with the simplicity of a meal that has a beginning, a middle and an end and that breaks through the superficiality of convenience food in the simple steps of beginning with raw ingredients, preparing and transforming them, and bringing them to the table. In this way we can again become freeholders of our culture.[32]

Last century, Borgmann described the intentionality it took to bring to awareness the significance of focal practices. A focal practice, then, is something that does not "scatter our attention" nor "clutter our surroundings." Thirty-five years later, the quality of our times must still be wrested from the digital landscapes that crowd our moments and often dictate our decisions. Intentional reading interrupts and invites us to breathe easier.

Reading is a cultural focal practice in renewal. For reading can always "clear a central place amid the clutter and distraction." And, we need to teach and learn a reading that intends to prepare for an encounter with the book in a way that can be still enough to recognize the beginning, middle, and end of reading. To reassert reading's focal character, its practical purpose of becoming mindful and attentive, to stop skimming and scanning and start encountering and exploring, we have to interrupt the digital pattern long enough to remember and renew the refreshing salience of solitude.

Consider just now books or articles you have read in the past that remain clear in your memory. Why are they there? When you thought of the book, what was it that you recollected? An image of the book? An image from the book? A quote, the smell of the book, what was pressing or significant about the environment or the context in which you read the book? In what way was reading that book enjoyable, or a struggle? Did the book confuse you at points? How did you work your way through the confusion? All

---

32. Borgmann, *Technology*, 204. For Christians, both the Word and the Sacrament are approached with deep intentionality and careful preparation. Thus, the quotidian and mundane necessities of eating and thinking are amplified.

these questions are merely an amplification of what happens when we read: inner dialogue. Inner dialogue is natural with reading, for as Borgmann has said: "The reader's world is diffuse and suggestive, while a virtual reality is definite and detailed."[33] In reading, we are inclined to a broad search; in the virtual world we are induced to scanning for particulars.

In the encounter with openness we experience our own emptiness, and very often it is filled with a lively inner dialogue. Are we open to the strange, constrained, perplexed, and abstract voices in our heads? When we reject or silence these contradictions we tend to close off a possible trajectory for thought. But if our habit is to keep the voices in a fluid conversation, we are able to see the intricacies of structure and structural connections among competing patterns. This is so much more than possessing information. When we read slowly it is as if consciousness is a laboratory, with an emphasis on *labor*atory. When you have a question for an author, whom do you ask first? The author, who tends to be unavailable, or yourself? The point is that open interest in ideas begins as a conversation with yourself. It is as though there are a multiplicity of identities within when you engage in an inner dialogue via literate encounter. Inner dialogue is necessary for open thinkers if for no other reason than you articulate a variety of factors and even understandings in an effort to discern the best among them. An open reader is always asking questions; some the text can answer, and we read along searching. Some are constantly asked and the most credible answer can only come from within. But we have to remain open. We are back to pattern and variability. In reading we recognize patterns of thought, even a pattern that has written into it a thousand tributaries. The variability we bring to that pattern opens out the possibilities of meaning and we can then discover novelty in the most mundane routine of reading. Taking time with reading, we open books carefully and attentively. But certainly books can also open us. In reading, we harbor and cultivate many ongoing encounters with thought. Learning and becoming open to wonder, the subject of our next chapter, we prepare a staple ingredient to the love of learning.

33. Borgmann, *Holding Onto Reality*, 91.

3

Wonder

"Most men do not think things in the way they encounter them, nor do they recognize what they experience, but believe their own opinions."

—Heraclitus

"Are we to encompass being with thought, or thought with being? In other words, are we to include the whole in one of its parts, or one of the parts in its whole?"

—Étienne Gilson

WONDER: DESCRIPTION

No one would deny the wonders of technology. The air balloon gave way to the glider, the glider to the plane, the plane to the drone, each form building from its predecessor, refining its structure while giving the human operators more control and broader powers of perception. We want to see; a "bird's-eye view" has never meant less. The internet is a wonder in that it induces a sense of awe while evoking interest in its use. The automatic door, the measuring and talking refrigerator, the responsive phone; these are wonder-full in the sense that they elicit ongoing action by confirming our innate curiosity. When we experience wonder in this way, we might be tempted by a utopian illusion. The air balloon need not have evolved into the drone, but it did in the context of war, of winning a war, and of minimizing death and destruction (a guarantee for the force with the drones). Technology develops in a complex and dynamic context, and drones were forged with a new vision of war in mind, one driven by the attempt to make war antiseptic and safer. This kind of wonder driving the utopian vision tends to narrow the scope of our vision. The tragedy and failure of war is still a tragedy and still a failure of diplomacy in spite of smart bombs and drone accuracy. In this case, the drone especially de-contextualizes our actions and *promotes* a simulacrum of violence, not the actual violence that inevitably results from drones. Let's take a look at a somewhat more benign, but no less forceful, example.

WONDER: GENERALLY OBSERVATIONAL

The iPhone that is an eye-phone. That phone responds to your individual and singular eye. And by your look, you are able to pay your bills, buy a shirt, get concert tickets, all by looking. What a wonder. The marketing team behind this operation is promoting nothing less than personalist metaphysics. That is, each human being is a singular, contingent, unrepeatable being, with traits distinct in kind. This eye-phone[1] is selling a truth. It is a truth affirmed by both evolutionary biology and Christian revelation. It certainly may make us wonder. Yet this truth is something some of us never come to know in our bodies. We tend only to play at it through consumerist preferences. In advertising, a radical contingency and a personal uniqueness are reduced to conformity in consumption. This is the case especially when competition is a factor. In the competitive condition, we feel a perceived necessity of consumption to secure our existential viability: tax-paying, upstanding, educated, legitimate. Aristotle calls this a good, the good of honor, but by itself it cannot lead to happiness.[2] This is the enduring work of marketing strategies, to offer us expressive answers to our contingency and insecurities. The face especially, the primary tool of human-to-human encounter, is sold back to us evoking that sensual memory of pattern and variability. If you watch an iPhone 10 commercial, you will see that, "with

1. I interchange iPhone and eye-phone here for poetic effect, nothing more.
2. Aristotle, *Nicomachean Ethics*, 98.

the blink of an eye" one can re-fashion themselves, attract a date, create chaos in the high-school hallways, and disrupt the biology lab. The ad reflects a truth. At the level of infancy this is true because of the critical work of the eye-to-eye encounter. The infant catching the parental eye has power over reality, can provoke in that large and loving being, a desired and sensuous response. Again, the wonder of the human face in encounter is sold back to us in its basest form. But, this marketing process is used to tell a lie. It is a lie in the sense that the eye-phone promotes a consumptive ideal in which there are no co-regulating parents to foster genuine relationality. The wonder-full experience of encounter gets ripped from the depth of its context. With this wondrous technological eye, the power of our eye, our I, is merely a refraction, a self-sealing feedback loop resulting in an impenetrable cell. And, after the wonder wears away, the I is alone and insecure in her or his consumption. Is it any wonder that there is a growing correlation between digital technology and adolescent depression?[3]

WONDER: BEING ENCOMPASSES MIND

The above-named technologies and especially the phone seem to me evidence of a major fallacy of the device paradigm. That fallacy assumes that the mind can both encompass and manipulate being. I hope that throughout our descriptions, our exemplification, and in the application of wonder-full encounter, we can unpack the reasons this fallacy has led to problems in thought and action. The digital culture and commodification promote the illusion that the mind encompasses being. Etienne Gilson has demonstrated that this fallacy became especially acute in the seventeenth century. We mistake a part for the whole. We mistake our theory, our perceptive grasp, our inflexible pattern, for the whole of reality. Citing Descartes' (1596–1650) important revolution in deductive certainty as an example, Gilson alerts us to the implications: "Everything will be mathematically proved in your philosophy, save only this, that everything can, and must be, mathematically proved."[4] Can you prove with deductive certainty that mathematical deductive proof is the best method of thought for every circumstance? Of course not. There is no doubt to the value of mathematical thinking. But when asked to prove that all thinking must be measured mathematically, we realize that there are other avenues for thought that

3. Twenge, "Has the Smartphone Destroyed a Generation?" 59.

4. Gilson, *Unity of Philosophical Experience*, 133.

might prove valuable as well, deliberations necessary to thinking clearly about the value of things in themselves. The modern period, valued for its astonishing gadgets and gizmos, data and drones, goes "from ideas to things" not "things to ideas."[5] To go from ideas to things is to see logs in a tree, to see $5,000 in a stately cherry. To go from things to ideas is to wonder at the tree's grandeur, origin, roots, presence. When mind wrongly assumes it can encompass being, we always think we know what we are looking at. The implication of this fallacy involves the assumption that the human mind's ability to understand reality entails garnering that knowledge for human ends, primarily consumption. The structure of encounter in this view places human experience primary and foremost. Nature, the universe, and in extreme cases, human others are secondary to the mind and its machinations. If this is true, wonder is an emotional experience, nothing more really. If mind encompasses being, wonder is certainly reduced. Wonder elicits focus in order to understand patterns and the value of nature and culture. Wonder involves a real attraction of understanding that draws our intellectual powers to an integral search. All the encounters in thought have deep value for our move toward knowledge and, importantly, our ongoing competence at asking the right questions. This is because the truth is actually an inversion of this fallacy, and the universe, nature, and others are something that encompass mind. Wonder is an experience of a surprising otherness, a some-thing encompassing us. So, when we see that being envelops mind, we are drawn to pursue being in its fullness and complexity. Wonder is the encounter in thought that facilitates this intellectual movement. This movement is dynamic, as we will see. Wonder involves a simultaneous awareness of the grandeur of being, along with a convivial call to offer one's own efforts at discovery.

ARISTOTLE: WONDER AND THE ETHOS OF DISCOVERY

The first sentence of Aristotle's *Metaphysics* is: "All men by nature desire to know." We especially become knowledge-able when we discover the cause of things. For a person to discover the cause of something, we move beyond the senses, we wonder. As Aristotle says, we can sense that the fire is hot, but to know why the fire is hot is another matter of the mind, a matter of wisdom.[6] The intellectual movement of discovering causes, the reason for

5. Gilson, *Unity of Philosophical Experience*, 153.

6. Aristotle, *Basic Works*, 689–90.

a thing's being, is not a pre-cast movement in efficient thinking. This kind of knowing cannot bring a pre-established format to the task of discovery. We have to let the things dictate our approach to them. The human gene pool is an example. Taken abstractly, the gene pool is mathematical in that it presents us with pattern and mechanism. In its operations, the gene pool appears to be random. When placed in the narrative structure of time, it leaves us with a wonderful sense of existential contingency. What is meant by contingency in this context is the truth that none of us chose to be here, to be born. Our lives are contingent on a complex, variable, series of events. We are, it seems, beings flowing on the whims of some arbitrary forces. This man, this woman, this date, this day, this night, this series of events, this kiss, that room, this sperm, that egg—this person, this life. One second later, bad breath, lack of chemistry, sober, and no person; at the very least, it gets us thinking. We wonder. We know the cause of life and birth, but we still wonder, sometimes in awe and gratitude, other times in despondency and sorrow. If we leave it there and move on into deterministic patterns of convention, we take it all for granted and we mitigate our innate desire to understand our place in the universe. But if we take the gene pool and history's minutiae as a part of a larger fusion of being, and we openly explore causes, wonder has done its job. But convention does persist, as does routine. That is why Aristotle clarifies the nature of wonder by saying that it is a result of non-utilitarian thinking; it is thinking when you have time to chase perplexity. It is thinking lovers of wisdom do when they have leisure. An extended quote will help here, Aristotle says it very well:

> For it is owing to their wonder that men both now begin and at first began to philosophize; they wondered originally at the obvious difficulties, then advanced little by little and stated difficulties about the greater matters, e.g., about the phenomena of the moon and those of the sun and of the stars, and about the genesis of the universe. And a man who is puzzled and wonders thinks himself ignorant[;] . . . therefore since they philosophized in order to escape from ignorance, evidently they were pursuing science in order to know, and not for any utilitarian end, . . . for it was when almost all the necessities of life and the things that make for comfort and recreation had been secured, that such knowledge began to be sought.[7]

7. Aristotle, *Basic Works*, 692.

Like openness, wonder requires time, and a disruption of the work-a-day world. Aristotle's quote brings to mind Borgmann's question regarding the best and the brightest. Since in the West, and in the U.S. particularly, we have the necessities of life "secured," should not four years of college be a training in the possible transformation of time? Not merely a respite from busyness to explore, but an exploration into the transposition of how work and time can be construed, an analysis of value related to ostensible success, consumption, and an engagement with nature in its urban, suburban, and rural ecologies? Basically, an intense exploration of the value of life, and the quality of life. At any rate, thinking for the sake of discovery is different from thinking for the sake of a desired outcome. So many businesses boast of innovation as a mark of their credibility. Meaningless products are the result of economics void of wonder. But innovation demands a training in wonder; the kind of persistent pursuit of a seemingly irrelevant question undertaken without the constraints of deadlines, grading criteria, and production schedules. Wonder is the beginning and end of thinking for its own sake. Elsewhere, Aristotle describes wonder as a coming into one's own, a sort of entry point into human intellectual flourishing. Since there is no limit to what we wonder about, wondering catches up our desire while utilizing both our powers of perception and our imaginations. Again, Aristotle, discussing the way persuasive speech ought to entice an audience's wonder, says:

> Learning things and wondering at things are also pleasant as a rule; wondering implies the desire of learning, so that the object of wonder is an object of desire; while learning one is brought into one's natural condition.[8]

What if what Aristotle says about our "natural condition" is true? I think it is. I suppose we would not read if we did not believe this at some level. Learning is enjoyable because of our experience of wonder, and more, learning is our natural condition. So, putting these Aristotelian teachings on wonder together; a life in wonder presents us with opportunities to interrupt our conventional conditions of utility. And those interruptions win for us time for exploration on its own terms. This is so that we might pursue our most essential human competency, learning. And this learning is something that we both desire and enjoy. But like openness, there is risk involved and it takes a commitment to intentional processes of observation,

8. Aristotle, *Basic Works,* 1365.

notably a belief that we are encompassed by a vast interconnected and complex structure of being/reality. And that reality is replete, and I what I mean by that is that there is always more to discover, even in our loved ones and ourselves. This intentionality takes intellectual risk and creativity, two aspects of being we cannot cultivate well if we are living spasmodically, trying desperately to become legitimate in a digital culture. Wonder: an integral experience of surprise, enjoyment, and perplexity.

As such, the experience of wonder promotes an interrogation of value, the value of the being that encompasses our minds, even our own being. Returning to the fact of human contingency, our wonder about the gene pool's randomness set against the context of human stories of love, attraction, and historical accidents presents to us an ultimate context and surprise. Wonder deepens our sense of life's value, or perhaps life's absurdity. Either way, in wonder deeper self-understanding usurps our pre-fabricated identities. Since the experience of wonder breaks open the self-enclosed certainty of our minds, we cannot take existence, our existence, for granted.[9] Nor can we take a tree's existence, or a tuna fish's, or McDonalds' French fries as merely given as a pre-proposed pattern for edifying my contingent being. A tree would be here if I weren't; a tuna-fish would be here, too. And French fries come from potatoes, damn it, and potatoes grow in the earth, an earth nourished by millennia of mineralization, rain, and volcanoes. A single rock tells the story of what nourishes me; the rock and I share a common story. I carry the minerals of the rock in my body. The rocks and stones call out for wonder too.

WONDER EXEMPLIFIED: EVA SAULITIS

"Sometimes we wish the world could cry and tell us about that which made it pregnant with fear-filling grandeur. Sometimes we wish our own heart would speak of that which made it heavy with wonder."

—ABRAHAM JOSHUA HESCHEL

Perhaps Aristotle was able to define the significance of wonder because he experienced it so often. After the death of his teacher Plato, Aristotle

9. Fuller, *Wonder: From Emotion to Spirituality*, 43.

returned to Athens to lead his own school, the Lyceum. There he began a new agenda for learning, becoming the lead researcher in the empirical methods inherited by Western science. In this, what Werner Jaeger has called his third period, he begins to investigate biological details, applying his conception of form to nature, initiating and confirming our current biological taxonomy of genus, species, etc. He does comparative political science by examining the constitutions of diverse states. He considers dreams in a new mode of inquiry, leaving their mystical meaning to explore their possible physiological cause. He collects facts and data from the field and compiles three works in biology, *The History of Animals*, *The Parts of Animals*, and *The Generation of Animals*.[10] He expresses a certain fascination with dolphins and whales, since they confound his established dualistic classification of terrestrial and aquatic animals.

> But the dolphin is equipped in the most remarkable way of all animals: the dolphin and other similar aquatic animals, including the other cetaceans which resemble it; that is to say, the whale, and all the other creatures that are furnished with a blow hole. One can hardly allow that such an animal is terrestrial and terrestrial only, or aquatic and aquatic only. . . . For the fact is the dolphin performs both these processes: he takes in water and discharges it by his blow-hole, and he also inhales air into his lungs; for by the way, the creature is furnished with this organ and respires thereby.[11]

Cetaceans are remarkable. The wonder we sense of their operations could be due to the human awareness of the life-giving powers of both water and air and the cetaceans' instinctual workings to balance these elements. Whales and dolphins are a wonder of evolutionary biology. The blow-hole represents the stewardship of vital powers that have been sorely compromised for the last two hundred years or so. How terrible it would be to slowly die for lack of air? And how terrible it would be to die of thirst? The spray from a blow-hole is also how biologist, poet, and writer Eva Saulitis first spotted orca transient whales in an Alaskan Sound, the ocean inlet that provided food and play to these cetaceans. The wonder that drove her science and poetry is recorded in her *Into Great Silence: A Memoir of Discovery and Loss*, where she describes her first eye-to-eye encounter with a wild orca as a baptism. It was 1987; she had volunteered to be a part of a crew identifying orcas off the shores of Alaska. A year later, she would be

10. Jaeger, *Aristotle*, 324–29.
11. Aristotle, *Works of Aristotle* vol. 4, 589.

in charge of a second research boat. On a skiff, assisting Craig Matkin, who logged photo IDs of orca fins and markings, Eva Saulitis encountered "an individual," she writes:

> One particularly fearless individual . . . —identified as female— lobbed her fluke a few feet from the bow, so hard it sent up spray. I ducked too late, then gasped, laughing. The frigid water on my face wasn't just any water. It was like holy water thrown at me by an aspergillum. I turned to Craig, overjoyed, but he looked uneasy. . . . For an hour and a half, she thwarted his efforts to photograph her left side. . . . Suddenly, the whale thrust herself straight up from the water, spy-hopping, so that her eye looked directly into mine. Blue. The iris was blue.[12]

Aspergillum—an implement for sprinkling holy water. In both the adult and infancy types of baptism carried out today in any number of churches, we can perceive the ideal type, an experience of wonder conjoining the emergence of joy, curiosity, and calling/vocation. Saulitis avails herself of this symbol in order to convey her truth: that in that joyous encounter with orca transients that day her scientific mind reawakened and her writing life was reborn. The waters integrated her disjointed twenty-three-year-old identity. Encounters in nature such as this are rare, but all encounters in nature evoke in us the sense that the environment heals us, that in being a part of larger networks of being, we are somehow found again in our storied place, a multi-layered insight into what is both true and possible. This is why Craig Whipkey's students thank him for making them prepare their own meal around a campfire without their digital devices. They become aware of their small but forceful capacity to be a part of a larger economy of truth and meaning.

For Saulitis, the experience of wonder integrated her analytic and emotional capacities. She expresses this experience, one we all undergo and then pursue at one time or another. Undergoing this thinking is an experience of learning how to learn, preserving our reason's skill in what seems like mind-juggling. "Watching the whales through the camera lens, the two hemispheres of my brain vied for dominance, one awash in wonder, the other struggling to memorize Craig's advice."[13] Because we are not open, focusing too much on codifying the pattern, we miss the opportunity to integrate what motivates our interest in the first place, we get frustrated with

12. Saulitis, *Into Great Silence*, 13–14.
13. Saulitis, *Into Great Silence*, 30.

what Saulitis calls the two hemispheres *vying*—we tend to let one or the other dominate. A scientist who is also a poet and writer never gives up the juggling struggle, and neither should we. Intellectual integration and self-trust is arduous and life-long. The two hemispheres have their corresponding religio-perceptual aptitudes: the left, analytical and critical, one could say prophetic; the right, receptive and aware, one could say sacramental.[14]

Eva Saulitis was certainly one of "the best and the brightest." In 1981 she won a scholarship to Northwestern University's conservancy, where she would study the oboe. She found the program to be "stifling, competitive, brutal."[15] Northwestern University sits on Lake Michigan, and one day as Eva looked out over the winter shore, she realized she did not have to live into this pattern, the one she found "stifling, competitive, and brutal." She went back to Western New York and earned a degree in wildlife biology at Syracuse University. She took a job at a fishery in Prince William Sound in Alaska, where she first saw an orca. After having volunteered with Craig Matkin, she would earn a master's degree in Zoology at University of Alaska, Fairbanks. She then returned to the same university to earn an M.F.A. in writing three years later.[16] The wonder that drove her life-long pursuits was the result of what she names as this "origin" moment. These are "firsts," moments when we transcribe every detail of the experience and through time, we can, as we say, "remember it like it was yesterday."[17] An origin moment keeps on giving, as it were, and we can begin to read our story through the lens of that moment. It opens us to our vocation. In the case of Eva Saulitis, notice how she was open enough to see how the particular pattern of the music conservancy was not a pattern in which she would thrive. Notice too that it was not the educational pattern that she resisted, having earned a degree in science. It was the *ethos* that drove that particular educational pattern.

Her talent as a musician would never go away, and we may suggest that her attraction to cetacean biology is in part due to their musical lives. The other remarkable thing about cetaceans that Aristotle does not mention is their culture of sound. Eva Saulitis' research on orca transients gives us a wonderful sense of their patterns of speech, their hunting and cultural

14. This is an induction drawn from David Tracy, he describes the juggling in a classic philosophic term, dialectic: see *The Analogical Imagination,* 203.

15. Byl, "Every Reason to Stay: Eva Saulitis's Life with Whales."

16. Byl, "Every Reason to Stay: Eva Saulitis's Life with Whales."

17. Saulitis, *Into Great Silence,* 19.

voices. Saulitis chose to study the transients as part of her graduate work. Orcas around the Alaskan shoreline come in at least two types, residents and transients. The transients come and go unexpectedly. Unlike resident orcas, who remain in their matrilines for life, transient orcas' social structure is more "fluid." "A transient might leave its matriline to join another, or disappear for several years, only to reappear." Eva Saulitis spent most of her adult life studying the gypsies of the cetacean world, gypsies who would resist the patterns of their resident orca cousins. Like gypsies, transients are "beat up, the trailing edges of their dorsal fins ragged, saddle patches scarred."[18] Transients sound different too. Saulitis' writing is filled with wonder, as she explains the first time she recorded transients:

> This was not the chatter of residents, the catlike whines and yips and whistles. This was something other: long, descending cries, and high intensity blasts ending in upsweeps, like questions. This was a voice at once strident and mournful, a strange hybrid instrument, part trumpet, part oboe, part elephant, part foghorn. And loud. In the calls' echoes, I imagined the passage mirroring back to the whales: *You are, you are.*[19]

Wonder's method of explanation is often analogy; it is new knowledge put on over well-worn sense experience; the sound of their particular song is an amalgam of instruments we think we know, and in trying to imagine the whale calls, we re-invent those instruments in our mind's ear. Later, her description becomes more analytic; having surveyed the research on transient calls, she informs the reader of the distinction between the types of calls. There are three call types: pulsed, whistles, and echo-location clicks. Interestingly, pulsed calls are mimetic; they are mimicked, "repeated over and over by all members of the pod." But the pulse can also be "aberrant," and, according to Saulitis, "whales turn their stereo-typed calls into playthings, warping familiar calls into barely recognizable variants." Whistles are like pulsed variants but are without harmonics. Whales have dialects, and significantly they learn to open up the patterns of their calls, as in improvisation. Saulitis says: "variable calls are pulsed, and, as far as we can tell, invented on the spot—random, one-time-only utterances—which is to say, we don't know much about them."[20] It is easy to see why Saulitis describes the female above as an individual. Like humans, whales play with their

18. Saulitis, *Into Great Silence*, 15, 17.
19. Saulitis, *Into Great Silence*, 39.
20. Saulitis, *Into Great Silence*, 53.

language, especially in celebration, after all have eaten, partaken communally of the kill. The third type of call is simple echo-location, putting out a signal and listening for how it comes back, discerning therefore what is probably ahead that the whale cannot see—boat, seal, fish, rock.

THE TRANSPOSITION OF THE ECOLOGICAL CONTEXT

Aristotle and Eva Saulitis share in the human experience of wonder. But their contexts are radically different. The difference that I want to stress is that our experience of nature today cannot but help being accompanied by what Rabbi Heschel calls a "heavy" wonder. Saulitis' wonder fueled her longing to search out and know these enigmatic creatures. In the presence of them, she could analyze patterns, like how long they stayed under water and the rhythm of their hunting routines. It was just that their presence was so very unpredictable. They seemed to appear and disappear without the more predictable migratory patterns of other cetaceans. As Saulitis emerged from her baptism, broader economic and technological patterns lurked and would prove cataclysmic for both orca transients and Eva Saulitis. She remarks: "The solitude and the silence of the Chugach transients—and the Sound—mirrored something inside me I didn't yet own. That knowledge would come much later."[21] *Into Great Silence* is a witness to that deep knowledge, and the wonder at life, death, and nature. Saulitis would witness the slow extermination of these transients due to the Exxon Valdez oil spill of 1989, which "spewed millions of gallons of crude oil into the Sound." By the time she wrote her master's thesis in 1993 there were only eleven Chugach transients left.[22] These transients had not re-produced since the spill. Was extinction an inevitability? And as she wrote her memoir, she was facing the destructive invasion of cancer in her body. That diagnosis was in 2010. The cancer would remit, but return in 2013, the year *Into Great Silence* was published. Death, too, is a wonder. But the possible extinction of the transients, and her own cancer, evoke in Eva Saulitis' writing and teaching a first-hand poetic and scientific account of our war against nature, including human nature. Our ecological context demands that we acknowledge and understand this culture of death, the death and resilience of nature, and our own singular undergoing of death, our solitude. Eva Saulitis can help us here. She can lead us into a heavier wonder of deep ecology.

21. Saulitis, *Into Great Silence*, 51.
22. Saulitis, *Into Great Silence*, 61, 197.

WONDERING: LISTENING FOR THE WORLD'S CRY

Thomas Merton teaches that we are together in our loneliness. This is because of death. Eva Saulitis' enduring reflections on the death of nature, her testimony to cancer's growth in her body, and her humble entrance into learning how to die, are a legacy of a heart that speaks with "fear filling grandeur." The amazing thing about Eva Saulitis' life, its wonder, is that she connected her vocational search for orca transients to her own process of "becoming earth." She would tell her colleague: "I also have a sense of wonder at how much we can't know. Orcas are like extraterrestrials to us." Like Aristotle, confounded by being that does not conform to our presumptions, she revels in the questions that inspire. "I think every dedicated scientist feels awe."[23] But a heavy question persists in her posthumous essays. In writing that offers to our death-denying culture a rare vulnerability, she wonders about the human capacity for denial. Why do we deny the foreboding, the inevitable, the possible storm of emotions that may be the sour fruit of our collective lie, our collective life? An oil spill killed thirty-six transient orcas, an entire pod. The ultimate implications of this are loss: of genetic diversity, a distinct way of orca life, a language, a culture.[24] The device paradigm helps us to forget; it motions to our habitual amnesic propensities and waves off our incisive awareness of "what is going on." Media ecology hides the gashes and scars in our deep ecology. I wonder, what happens to a culture that never mourns its losses? Unless we begin to wonder about the patterns of distraction, we cannot penetrate the way all our consumptive culture yields quite devastating unintended consequences.

Saulitis' wonder about it all turns inward, describing in *Becoming Earth* her experience with denial about a lump in her breast she has discovered. In acknowledging her denial, she is teaching us about how to face the ultimate question, the wonder of our own living and dying. When she felt the "peach pit" in her breast her whole body knew, "malignancy." She confesses: "All the *knowing* happened in less than a second. And then I'd risen back out of my body and into my head, and say to myself, 'No, you are paranoid . . . this is not your story.'"[25] Eva Saulitis witnesses to her own process of denial and in doing so she teaches us that denial only comes

---

23. Byl, "Every Reason to Stay: Eva Saulitis's Life with Whales," 8.

24. Byl, "Every Reason to Stay: Eva Saulitis's Life with Whales," 8.

25. Saulitis, *Becoming Earth*, 10 (emphasis mine).

after an encounter with concrete knowing. It is an embodied knowing. It is a knowledge of the tangible life-world that encompasses our minds at every turn. She helps us to see that some of our thinking is an escape from being, an escape from the bios; we escape through reason to confirm the stories we have already fleshed out and appropriated, to escape into the well-worn patterns of thought. Notice how she describes it. She rose "into her head." That is a way of saying that our default cultural pattern presumes that mind encompasses being. That pattern is instantiated over and over again in the technological and digital patterns that determine our automated responses to most of life's situations. Learning this, Saulitis warns us all about how we might approach death. She wonders, what ought we really fear?

> I know that as long as we inhabit bodies of flesh, blood, and bone, we are wholly inside nature. . . . Flesh, blood and bone not-with-standing, a body hooked by way of tubes to suction devices, by way of an IV needle to a synthetic morphine pump forgets its organic animal self. In the hospital, I've learned to fear something more than death: existence dependent upon technology, machines, sterile procedures, hoses, pumps, chemicals easing one kind of pain only to feed a psychic other.[26]

When Eva Saulitis returned to Prince William Sound to research orcas the year of the Exxon oil spill, she was "terrified of two things: the presence of oil and the absence of life."[27] Facing the truths that confirmed her fears, she began to see that the corporate and governmental collusion, the technocracy that acted without the urgency she felt in her bones, was just as crude and invasive as the oil. She and her colleague would write an editorial for the local paper about the technocratic pattern.

> When we walk the beaches, we can hear that community (of invertebrates) speaking, trying to breathe under a black blanket of poison. Equally disturbing is the human occupation, the domination and scouring of this poisoned wilderness. . . . The relentless activity has the feeling of war, dramatized by the presence of military personnel carriers and landing craft. . . . Already one grizzly bear

---

26. Saulitis, *Becoming Earth*, 69. Saulitis describes intuitively what Jeffrey P. Bishop describes philosophically about palliative care. See his examination of how pain management has developed historically, becoming the techno-pharmacological science of death, *The Anticipatory Corpse: Medicine, Power and the Care of the Dying*, 253–64.

27. Saulitis, *Into Great Silence*, 64.

has been shot in the sadly ironic defense of Exxon's beach crews as they try to remove oil before wildlife gets slimed.[28]

The routines and patterns of technological efficiency aid in our denial, our encounter with the truth of what our collective life has wrought. In healthcare and earth care, the technocratic pattern runs ahead of the human and natural contexts of dying and cleaning up after disaster. The fixing, the expertise, the project, the startling new method, newer tech efficiency, the gathering of arms/pharma for safety, the best practices, the parade of missed deadlines and staid responses, the marketing, the euphemisms for/about death, destruction, the spin. The pattern asserts itself in trying to undo itself. A saner solution is to desist. This, at least for a moment, might allow the induction of wonder to situate itself. Saulitis also wonders about her upbringing along Lake Erie in western New York's southern tier. Her "body's encounter with that very landscape, that very backyard lake water tainted with DDT, pesticide sprayed on vineyard or U-pick strawberry field or all over my father's apples trees by his own hand." She wonders, could this be the reason for the tumor's growth?[29] Like other scientists, notably Sandra Steingraber, Saulitis infers a possible connection between the body, its native environment and disease. The implication is that if anyone is getting sick and the probable cause is the use of toxic substances for efficient economic gains, then we ought to attend to alternatives.

Saulitis exemplifies a wonder-full life because questioning and truth-telling are intransigent modes of her scientific heart and poetic mind. Saulitis conveys this wonderful truth: that death and nature have their own otherness and remain enigmatic and resilient. Both of them prompt surplus: to saturate our spongy minds and our thirsty imaginations with wonder. Both nature and death resist our mind's grasp. Eva Saulitis' wonder led her to these profound conclusions, a result of an encounter she had on a hike, through a creek, observing hundreds of dead, dying, or spawning salmon. In an essay first published just under two years before her death in 2016, she encourages us with these words:

28. Saulitis, *Into Great Silence*, 74–75.

29. Saulitis, *Becoming Earth*, 13. See also Sandra Steingraber, *Living Downstream*, 64. Steingraber notes that absolute proof in science is very rare, and that, we have to infer some connection. There is no doubt, however, about the contaminants involved in many businesses, including dry-cleaning, which Steingraber cites as dangerous. Her book examines cancer maps, and she notes that the Great Lakes basin is a red zone for breast and bladder cancer due to its industrialized history.

> Death is nature. Nature is far from over. In the end, the gore at the creek comforts more than it appalls. In the end—I must believe it—just like a salmon, I will know how to die, and though I die, though I lose my life, nature wins. Nature endures. It is strange, and it is hard, but it is comfort, and I'll take it.[30]

The beguiling quest of life begins and ends in wonder.

WONDER APPLIED: WALKING

Saulitis hiked, not because she was doing field work, but rather to take a break from her oceanic work. She hiked to be enveloped by life in its diversity. Walking has always been at the heart of discovery. Aristotle's nickname was *the walker*, perhaps because he was purported to pace while he lectured, but also, his school was located in what was formerly a gymnasium, and there was a sort of walking track there, the place the master and disciples would meet. Aristotle's school of walkers bequeathed to the Western tradition the somewhat paradoxical intersection of the call to introspection through the medium of walking out-of-doors. In walking we are transposed, going inside-out and outside-in. Philosophy distinguishes itself by its beginnings in bi-pedal movement. Socrates walked about the city. His goal was not so much to encounter nature but to encounter and interrogate others, human nature, all kinds of people he wanted to learn from. Immanuel Kant is said to have walked at the same time each day, a pattern that never changed, 5:00 p.m.[31] Nietzsche was suspicious of sedentary learners, and hiked his whole life, until his health would not let him pursue the out of doors anymore.[32] And, of course, Henry David Thoreau, the precursor to John Muir and Rachel Carson and the father of American civil disobedience, wrote an essay on walking.[33] Most dramatically, walking convenes political movements. Think of the march on Washington, for example (1963). Walking is thinking's pump; we walk to learn, re-learn, discover, and expand. Ambling and wonder go hand in hand.

---

30. Saulitis, *Becoming Earth*, 75.

31. Gros, *A Philosophy of Walking*, 153–58. I have relied on Gros' very readable and enjoyable book and my own experience for these reflections.

32. Gros, *A Philosophy of Walking*, 11.

33. Gros, *A Philosophy of Walking*, 87–88.

OUTSIDE: MORE THAN UTILITARIAN TUNNEL

Conditions of modern existence make the outside a mere space between insides. We go from inside to inside, from home to market, from home to school, from home to work. And for many of us, that involves sitting with a circle in our hands inside an auto. And many of us get out of the seats in our cars, and walk into a place where we sit for a majority of the day. Walking outside is just a space between insides. Walking in this space is a utilitarian exercise, and, as Frédéric Gros has said, outside almost becomes an obstacle, having little value of its own.[34] But outside is not merely a space; it is *place*. Though we often use the terms interchangeably they are very distinct designations. And an encounter with place gets us thinking qualitatively. Space is basically measurable by quantity. Space is longitude/latitude, it is miles, feet, square-feet, kilometers, etc. This means that space is over-come, traversed, surmounted. When thinking and walking, three of reason's distinct aspects are employed. First, when walking we traverse space, so quantitative operations become implicit, our bodies measure the fourth dimension in our motion. Second, when we begin to become part of a place, our analytic operations are employed; we see relationships of material to social, of parts to wholes, of pattern and novelty. Third, we employ the intuitive and interpretive, developing the inevitably subjective "sense" of a place.

Place is perceived more holistically. We recognize the qualities of a place. Walking convenes our reason; it is an integrative prospect. Space is utilitarian, a tunnel to another inside. We enter and dwell in places. Places envelop us, even as we move through them. When walking, we go outside to enter places and become a part of them.[35] Automatic and predictable, we move through space to get somewhere. But when we walk without agenda, our physical movement is but a catalyst to mental movement: we wonder. For example, in walking, we become aware of the limited angle of our observational equipment, and as we move the landscape begins to reveal itself to us in its structure and layered diversity. Our inquiry sharpens as we move: What is up ahead? Around the bend? Will it rain? Perception of space and time become sharpened too. Again, we know concretely distances in relation to our physical capacities. We stop to observe the time it takes a squirrel to cross the electric line. Our motion is more attuned to

34. Gros, *A Philosophy of Walking*, 31–32.
35. Tuan, *Space and Place*, 12.

time's passing because our legs measure and sound off, in rhythm to our wondering and judgments. And we may also begin to notice debris along the way. Evidence of consumptive addiction lies along the side of the road, outside the purview of our automatic windows/windshields. Walking, we are more attuned to both space and place.

MEANDERING ALONG

Some, like Nietzsche, thought that walking with others threw off the tangential course of wandering. It is all about *pace*. Like a group of students working on a project, one pupil begins to lead and sets the pattern, while others simply follow along, passively. In deciding to walk without agenda, we enter the pace of our own bodies in motion, our breathing, our senses. We slowly enliven the intellect's vantage points. Being outside we live more intentionally; as it were, within. Walking is a foundational pattern of movement. Thinking again of infancy and "toddler-hood," walking is the first embrace of freedom, limbed gifts for more intensive searching. If we enter the outside, expecting to undergo its provocations in replete-ness; from dirt to sky and back again, we pace our observations by our steps. If in our "regularity of paces" we perceive a "mountain skyline" that stays with us for a few miles, we "stretch time." Gros explains: "It is one of the secrets of walking: a slow approach to landscapes that gradually renders them familiar. Like the regular encounters that deepen friendship."[36] Walking without agenda, at our own pace, ruptures the pervasive expectations of utility. Think of walking along the beach, or to the top of a mountain or a hill. What is the feeling there? That feeling is situated by the vista, the openness in places rendering to us the possibility of something different, good, and new. It is in walking to that point of observational expanse that a deep sense of presence is promoted. Why? Because you know how you got there, you know where you are, and you see what is ahead. This is a deep and embodied knowing, the mind's unique gait forged through the walk. Wonder gets us moving; there is really no other way to possess, or be possessed, of such knowledge. The embodied knowing Eva Saulitis carried into her river walk made her especially receptive to the meaning of spawning salmon. Her wonder opened the vantage point of receptivity: Trout know how to die. No one has to tell them or assuage their process. If trout know how to die, perhaps I can endure this knowing too, I can enter that process by way

36. Gros, *A Philosophy of Walking*, 36–37.

of wonder. Does it take existential crisis or an extraordinary experience to become receptive? Let's be receptive to the notion that receptivity is both a conditioned intellectual virtue, and evidence of genuine emotional care. Let's at least be receptive to the possibility that we might think about the meaning of receptivity in a new light. That is the goal of the next chapter.

4

Receptivity

"When a teacher asks a question in class and a student responds, she receives not just the "response" but the student. What he says matters, whether it is right or wrong, and she probes gently for clarification, interpretation, contribution. She is not seeking the answer but involvement of the cared for."

—NEL NODDINGS

RECEPTIVITY: DESCRIPTION

RECEPTIVITY IS THE MOST explicitly educational encounter in thought. In this way, it is the *epitome* of each encounter we describe. The feature of receptivity shared by all other encounters is receiving. We undergo reception. This aspect of learning through encounter represents all encounters as potential gift. Note that our analytical judgments are exercised, confirmed, and made competent as a result of parsing the gift, the person, or idea that has been *given*. Perhaps $2x + 3 = 7$ does not look like a gift. But, in the receptive solitude prior to the analytic operation, the algebraic symbols invite to reveal the unknown! It is the mode of discovery that is received most enduringly, an experience of thought that remains vital long after we scribble $x=2$. Receiving the algebraic, we become more confident in our search for all sorts of unknowns.

An encounter in thought, receptivity involves a matrix of four distinct experiences. The first two, what I will call the mind's micro-economy, are the relatedness between our experiences of thinking and our thinking about experiences. Our educational ethos has tended to accentuate the latter and ignore or reject the former. The other two in the matrix of receptivity are what I call the mind's macro-economy of relatedness. The third point on the matrix is easily neglected in our educational structure. It is the fundamental identity of the teacher as a representative of the ethical ideal of caring. The encounter with others as receptivity is a formative catalyst for the fourth experience in the matrix of receptivity, the reception of ideas that cultivate the dynamic synergy between perceiving-receiving, judgment, and analysis. Though we can distinguish between these experiences of relatedness, we acknowledge that learning through the quality of receptivity is analogous to the quadratic. R=receptivity, ET=experience of thinking, TE=thinking about experience, RT=receptivity of teacher/other, RI=receptivity of ideas, T= time, multiple times of experiences. Each within the quadratic can be measured by degrees of negative and positive. This symbolic exponentiation allows us to appreciate the relational complex of receptivity. $R = (\pm ET \text{ x} + TE)^{\wedge}T + (\pm RT \text{ x} \pm RI)^{\wedge}T$ [1]

As epitome, receptivity convokes the structure of intellectual conversion. As we mature, we find those factors in encounter that yield the qualities necessary for deeper understanding. If we work descriptively and break the equation into its more explicitly linguistic frame, I am suggesting that in each encounter of formal learning we measure and embody:

A. *The mind's micro-economy of relatedness*

    1. Our experience of thinking

    2. Thinking about our experience

B. *The mind's macro-economy of relatedness*

    1. Perceptual/reception of teacher/other

    2. Reception of idea/concept

---

1. This abstraction is simply an attempt to show the complex aggregations involved in four aspects of receptivity. Noddings suggests there is a logic to receptivity, but she does not want to "make the move to abstraction that tends to destroy the caring itself." Noddings, *Caring*, 33. I run the risk of doing that only to convey a holistic structure and variability. Perhaps so we see that all minutiae of educational encounter carries the weight of the ethical ideal.

The word *economy* is meant to express that sense of stewarding the household. A household is constituted by a daily engagement of many encounters that measure, conserve, preserve, and also change or shift varied material and spiritual pieces making up a whole. An economy of receptivity helps us to understand the prospect of learning as a stewarding. Wisdom comes, I believe, by way of refining our competency in understanding those relationships in their reasonable aspect. In this somewhat mystifying way, we note that there is an integrating energy/operation at work. I don't want to call it an ego, still less a self, but a rational integration that guides and acts to aggregate these experiences richly. This personality, both forging and receiving, is the structure strengthened or mended prior to, and after, human encounter. I may call this integrating aspect mind; or rather, minding. When we allow mind its adverbial reference, we more accurately express the mystery here.[2] The fact of receptivity makes me reluctant to use more static descriptions of self or ego because they fail to command the truth of our synergistic and integrative learning experience, the learning person. At any rate, that learning is contingent upon becoming receptive in these four modes. Let us take each mode, one by one, and thereby connect and clarify receptivity.

RECEPTIVITY AND OUR EXPERIENCE OF THINKING

Receptivity involves intending a conscious grasp of our thinking, we can call that developing awareness. An example of the conscious role of receptivity in awareness can be demonstrated as we consider what is happening when we ask a question. Questioning is an experience that has a definite pattern or process we can either refine or ignore. Our experience of a question places us in a particular mental condition. There are three aspects of this condition. First, when we enter the question we possess partial knowledge of something. This knowing in part is a discovery that our experience is somehow incomplete. Secondly, we become *aware* of our partial knowledge, our ignorance. And third, we come to a deeper awareness that there is something more to be known.[3] I want to focus on the awareness in the second and third aspects. For when we become aware of something we just don't know, or understand, it is possible to reject or fearfully recoil from

2. Minding habitually (i.e., in a pattern) is different from minding carefully. The adverbs help us appreciate the rich and varied process.

3. Reichmann, *Philosophy of the Human Person*, 12–13, 22.

this awareness. There are ways our prior experience may form this fear, the reception of browbeating and its concomitant shame. It may also be relational: a parent or teacher enclosed in cultural or individual presumptions is received. Or, it could be a relationship with television, internet, or digital addiction, perhaps a more intransigent habit-forming structure. In the experience of the question's partial knowledge, we *entertain* the knowledge that is revealed in the asking of the question. Do birds recycle? If, on a walk, my seven-year-old asks this question, he already knows what recycling is; he knows that birds populate his life-world with sound and flight. He sees and hears bird communities feeding, foraging, and fighting. He knows what the general shape of recycling looks like, taking used matter and offering it for renewal of purpose. A counter-question, a rhetorical one no doubt, is: where do birds live? We may begin talking about trees and nests and homes and recycling twigs, dirt, and litter to create a dwelling place. All this is done, of course, without a search engine. The "search engine" is initiated by *his own reception* of his question and its thick awareness of what he already has experienced of birds, of recycling. And further, it is my experience of his question and *my reception* of its creative intelligence. The seven-year-old's experience of his own question is an encounter in receiving and enlarging the awareness of his curiosity. An encounter with an iPad and an ornithology website cannot have the same provocation of this awareness, and neither can an encounter with an adult who laughs or berates the seven-year-old's awareness, his question.

Our experience of thinking can cultivate awareness. Innate deductive and inductive intelligence, the so-called I.Q., the symbol and criterion for "smarts" in modernity, certainly is important. However, those capacities have often de-emphasized the significance and enjoyment of our thinking experience; an awareness that evolves as an alert engagement and receptivity of our questions, our quest. Finding information is one thing. We can all develop the skill of piling up bits and facts to remember. But cultivating awareness is the preface to deeper knowing. It is also the prerequisite to responsibility. This is so because awareness is knowledge of *our knowledge* as pursued, received. We have earned it and therefore ideas seep deeply into our experience, standing under all future experiences. We receive and take this understanding into every other encounter. It is an integrating prospect. In a court of law, the degree of our understanding of wrongdoing provides the criterion for blame. In the experience of inquiry, we are cultivating a reception of personal responsibility. When a seven-year-old infers that a robin chick could choke on thin plastic cigarette wrappers, he may see litter in an entirely different way.

RECEPTIVITY AND THINKING ABOUT OUR EXPERIENCE

Notice how the experience of the seven-year-old's question presents a sense of relationality and belonging. In thinking about experience we develop concepts. "I have a place, the birds have a place. I re-use things, the birds re-use things." The receptivity of our questions draws us into the receptivity of a conceptual process: we relate to a world of which we are a part, we belong to a structure, a pattern we can consider and explore. We think, and re-think, our experience in belonging. Belonging fastens our mind onto receptivity of ideas. In belonging we don't stand over and against. We enter the question, we receive the ideas; then and only then, do we manipulate them. If we should think about experience without receiving our questions, we are apt to conclude that the purpose of thinking is simply to overlay our presumptions onto reality. We go from inside to inside. Nature, or the "outside," is nothing more than a tunnel to the artifice of my job, my building, my hardware store, my church. Thought projections are not receptive; they pursue information as if the mind can encompass being. Receptivity or reception of that sense of belonging to a particular place, a region, a nation, infuses subsequent learning. In this way, nature is not an abstract concept, but a living dynamic of which we are a part: in the city, in the country, in the suburbs, in the national park. And thus, we are receptive to nature's system, its eco-system.

More questions can incite the move from our experience of thinking to thinking about experience. With Robert Sokolowski, we inhabit a conceptual quarry when we ask a simple question. (Is it raining?) We move back and forth between our experience of thinking and thinking of experience in pursuit of our participation in a broader manifestation of what is real. When we say "It is raining," to what does the "it" refer? Let us rest to receive this question. In the question we receive the unspecified "it," and implicate ourselves relationally: when *it* is raining, nothing in particular is raining, *everything* is. Here, as Sokolowski has it, the "verbal manifestation predominates."[4] As *the* verb among all other active motion, being asserts its holistic structure. By saying, *it* is raining, "this impersonal construction . . .

4. Sokolowski, *Presence and Absence*, 17–18.

implies that we do not generate the thoughts and appearances we have, but that they come to us." Two things: there is a pattern we cannot manipulate and we can interpret and be a part of that pattern. When "it" is raining, we come to realize and receive the truth that we are environmentally constituted. Despite the umbrella, we enter an ecostructure, the "it" that encompasses even as we resist being part of the whole.

The receptive ones describe it thus: *a thought just came to me.* Shall we think of it through the ideas so predominant today? How about evolutionary biology? What is the purpose of receptivity in the economy of survival of the fittest and adaptation? The assumption may be that in human survival, analytic manipulation supersedes all other modes of thought. In organizing and leveraging data, I become successful; as a business, I survive, even thrive. As the ecological crisis mounts, we realize that this paradigm cannot be sustained. In fact, it is only in receptivity that we can truly understand the limits of human ingenuity and the persistence and resilience of nature. In the evolution of the human experience of thinking, receptivity persists to upend reason's sense of control and manipulation. As such it enchants our experience with the humble permissiveness of child-like perception. Receptivity is an activity through which we integrate thinking about experience with our experience of thinking. It can thus enliven our moral sense.

RECEPTIVITY AND THE MUTUAL ENCOUNTER OF CARE: ENGROSSMENT

We care about our questions, and we begin to care about the concepts that enlarge our awareness. The pathos of learning must traverse the path of receptivity. At its root, care is feeling. But that feeling grows conscious of itself through knowledge. The receptive encounter is concrete, not in any way abstract. The care-feeling invites the care-giver. It is an invitation to see things from an alternative perspective.[5] Atop the chapter is a quote from Nel Noddings, a philosopher who opened a new door in ethics by making receptivity the touchstone of her educational proposal.[6] She describes the

5. Noddings, *Caring*, 32.

6. Noddings' *Caring* was published two years after Carol Gilligan's ground-breaking *In a Different Voice*. By placing care ethics into the classical philosophical conversation, Noddings' work has impacted moral philosophy. Ethicist Michael Slote has taken up receptivity in terms of re-framing our values; Slote credits Noddings for his new emphasis. The great impact of care ethics has led Noddings to say that "given the scope of current work on care ethics, it probably is no longer appropriate to label it a 'feminist' ethic."

receptive encounter between teacher and student not only as feeling, but there is another aspect: "a motivational shift" in energy.[7] This Noddings calls *engrossment*. I want to consider three aspects to this based on word derivation. "Gross" has many meanings dating to Middle English and Latin. One that is still used is "something that can be seen with the naked eye," as opposed to microscopic. Hence, biology students must take gross anatomy in order to know the structure of the body. Gross is not a squinting to concentrate on fragmented parts. So, it has the sense of entire and whole, as in the income that is untaxed, not separated, the gross income. It is a grasp of what is given. It is not a partial grasp, as if parts have been extracted or distracted for other purposes. Third, it refers to that which is material and perceptible, not ethereal. Gross is tangible, and in that sense obvious. In engrossment, therefore, we have a perceptual palate based upon the encounter with another through which presence is given—that is, perceived holistically—and it is fundamentally concrete. Finally, gross has been a verb, a verb now obsolete by itself, but given to our educational philosophy as *engrossment*. Engrossment is the action of encounter that solicits the whole person; all the mental faculties are mobilized by the feeling of care. Nel Noddings, who first described engrossment as an ethical ideal in *Caring,* has refined her definition in a later book on the philosophy of education. This refinement distinguished pedagogical engrossment from more superficial engagements with students:

> I've called this receptivity "engrossment," but that term is not meant to suggest infatuation, obsession or single-mindedness. It suggests, rather, a nonselective form of attention that allows the other to establish a frame of reference and invite us to enter it. . . . [T]his is always a sensitive task that involves total receptivity, reflection, invitation, assessment, revision, and further exploration.[8]

By calling this approach "non-selective" I believe Noddings is helping us to see a presence not only available, but ready to be prevailed upon, in the sense of a non-selective awareness of the multidimensional presence of the student, his whole being. There is never a straight line from the teacher modeling the ethical ideal to the students' reception of ideas. No, many times, an intelligent person, having not been received by teachers or parents, will jump to ideas and become engrossed in the enjoyment of

---

Philosophy of Education, 236.

7. Noddings, *Caring* 33.

8. Noddings, *Philosophy of Education*, 238.

learning precisely because they do not enjoy thinking about their experiences of rejection, or their experience of their teachers being dismissive of their presence. Our point here, however, is that Noddings' description of engrossment provides a concrete exemplification of the caring encounter of receptivity. We turn, as it were, "with the naked eye of our hearts" to another. Also, engrossment calls upon the whole person, particularly in terms of their full presence, i.e., *undistracted*. In this encounter, the gross income of our mental powers is leveraged in engrossment toward the cared for. Listen again to Noddings: "When a teacher asks a question in class and a student responds, she receives not just the 'response' but the student."[9] Students perceiving the teacher engrossed in them evolve a reciprocity that induces intellectual growth and ultimately a reception of ideas as distinct and alive.

RECEPTIVITY AND CARING ABOUT IDEAS

What is at stake when we encounter new ideas? Let's turn Noddings' comment about teachers receiving students on its head. When a student listens and is receptive to a teacher's presence (of criticism, skepticism, or partisanship) they become receptive to a very narrow view of reason's fundamental task. This is precisely why the classical role of philosophy cannot give way to either Marxist or Libertarian assumptions, even though both philosophies convey powerful insights. The classical role of philosophy is one of interrogation, not system-building. And the presumption of having philosophy at the foundation of liberal arts curricula is to give people access to the tools of their own minds, not to convince them of liberalism's effacement or power. Both teaching and learning must be receptive to divergent ideologies. It is a matter of moral responsibility. Put simply, persons have no right to critique what they have never taken time to understand/receive. Studying trigonometry, reading a novel, or translating Spanish, take time for the full regimen of our reason to be deployed. Unlike receiving the listing provided by search engines or gleaning data from websites, sustained attention, engrossment with ideas and concepts, takes time. Our receptive competence is the intellectual virtue necessary to come to the truth in all its expressions, scientific, religious, and philosophic. Each of these are culturally bound, have a long and storied tradition, and aggregate historical findings even as they learn from each other. The educated person cannot claim

9. Noddings, *Caring*, 176.

that name badge unless they can both receive and adjudicate diverse and oft-times dichotomous notions. Previous philosophers are always helpful here, since they elaborate on questions that remain pressing. This is why the role of the teacher in this process is so very profoundly important. A good teacher is generously receptive of great ideas while acknowledging that those ideas are not the "final answer." A teacher's consistent performative receptivity can result in a student turning on the filter as the mind watches a stream of ideas pour in. Without that modeling, receptivity can let everything in without judgment's filter. That can result in students becoming frustrated and then concluding that moral or cultural relativism is "true"; although, their use of the word "true" confounds them when we ask how they arrived at that "conclusion." The claim that relativism is the way things are is known *how?* How is it that you know relativism is true? since everything is relative to me and my culture, I cannot even understand what you *mean* by the word truth! I might say to students, "But of course, it *is* true that we are talking, right? So we have some basis for continuing to pursue truth in its objective aspect, do we not?" Digital habits only serve to compound a student's experience of confusion due to hyper-receptivity. The fallacy of moral and cultural relativism alongside of the digital habits of culture, mitigates the engrossment necessary for searching and researching truth. So, filter-less receptivity, an encounter of disingenuous engrossment, can result in students being easily manipulated by all sorts of propaganda, advertisements, and "the latest scientific study."

TRUTHFUL RECEPTIVITY IN THE RECEPTIVITY OF TRUTH

To sum up: for the sake of our argument, let us propose that before we think about our experience, we experience our thinking. When we think about our experience we may recollect our learning; we receive that recollection as good, bad, indifferent, or some combination of those. But as a preface to that, I suggest, we experience our thoughts, and this involves undergoing the complex of emotion and reason. Receptivity is the engrossed elongation of that undergoing in relatedness: our experience of thinking to our thinking about experience, our receptivity of another to our receptivity of ideas. Think of opening a gift. Unwrapping slowly, in anticipation, takes patience and studied focus for discovery. If the experience of our thinking develops in insecurity of being received, or fear of being rejected, when we get around to thinking about our experience of learning, we re-enter that negatively appropriated complex. We may therefore fail to become receptive to our questions, to the unknowns that lurk throughout our experience. We then default, preferring the irate tirade in digital to the reasonable encounter of conversation. This may happen especially when our awareness is unaccompanied by affirmations of our intelligence. The worst thing that can happen in learning is that our questions become for us a sign of our inadequacy rather than our strength.

Michael Slote has suggested that a renewal of receptivity is necessary precisely because thinking about ecology is intrinsically a receptive mode of inquiry.[10] This "green thinking" is not, unlike modernity's rational legacy, an attempt to surmount nature through control and manipulation. It is, rather, receptive of both nature's and culture's dynamic inter-relations. Nature is given, studied for its own unfolding. Culture is received and understood, in its wonderful historical unfolding. Conserving and preserving both nature and culture demands that we think less about the goal of efficiency and more about reason's sufficiency, whereby we understand what is given. Receptivity's end is truth, existential truth, the kind of truth that transforms our lives should we receive it, perceive it, and pursue it. Ultimately appropriating truth will set us free so that we can begin to take our place in the healing of both nature and culture. But, because time makes brittle reason's patterns, our receptivity could cease to move along the quadratic, or that negatively. Each encounter renews the potential resolve to open ourselves through the dynamic of receptivity. Both negative forces or a schematic overindulgence of positive forces can serve to make us unreceptive to our natural inclination for intelligibility, for truth. But for others, the capacity for receptivity is persistent, for truth has been amplified in the reasoning-experiential process. Receptivity is the whisper that eventually forms a high decibel shout as truth becomes the substance contained in every encounter of thought. For an exemplification of receptivity, the search and expression of truth, we turn to Malcolm X, one of the most dynamic purveyors and conveyers of truth the twentieth century ever heard. At the end of his life, when he was certain he would be assassinated, Malcolm X predicted that white folks in America would take over his image and cast his legacy in a negative light. Such a prediction was based on his own engagements with American whites, blacks, and the press. The "press," now digital media, emulsifies and whips up such sensationalist vagaries and

10. Slote, *From Enlightenment to Receptivity*, 181–93.

versions of truth. I want to suggest that, to a very great degree, his prediction seems to have been accurate. And resistance to the Black Lives Matter movement only confirms that truth. His accurate prediction is a reflection not only of Malcolm X's insight, but a reflection of the shallow, superficial, and consumerist culture that has continuously eroded healthy patterns of coming to terms with reality. In the words of Malcolm X Shabazz:

> I do not expect to live long enough to read this book in its finished form—I want you to just watch and see if I'm not right in what I say: that the white man, in his press, is going to identify me with "hate." He will make use of me dead, as he has made use of me alive, as a convenient symbol of "hatred"—and that will help him to escape facing the truth that all I have been doing is holding up a mirror to reflect, to show, the history of unspeakable crimes that his race has committed against my race.[11]

Is that not the problem of learning, from elementary school to marital discord to social and political wrangling, the *escape* from truth? The escape from the brute facts of history? The amnesia, such a persuasive force in American optimism, that can never escape from the past evils of history: in the comforts of fragmented and cellular existence, those truths begin to appear scurrilous to the comfortable. Receptivity to truth, engrossment to the realities that captivate culture, is the only way to move out of illusion. The "mirror" does not lie.

Being receptive, we seek to become engrossed in the facts as understood by Malcolm X, his frame of reference. We can say the same for the facts of the eventual depletion of oil, that the poor receive the ugly brunt of the U.S.'s voracious appetite to consume and ravage nature, that plastic may be on the planet longer than human beings will. We are interested in Malcolm X not only because of his diagnosis of the condition of white America as unreceptive to truth, but also because we want to appreciate whatever it is that prompts us to "escape" the truth.

Malcolm X's foresight was due to a truth he discovered in childhood. It is the truth that the white power structure, or those institutions of power, will apply every moral criterion to those who challenge them, but they will never apply that same criteria to themselves with the same intensity or with the same punitive outcome. Whether this is the human condition, or the condition of whites in America, is perhaps another philosophical question. The point is, whoever is in this condition of denial is unreceptive, and that

11. Malcolm X, *The Autobiography of Malcolm X as Told to Alex Haley*, 439.

wreaks havoc. The havoc of chronic hypocrisy is something one wants to separate from, to live as far away as one can from that destructive force. The force of denial is wielded by a pattern, and, just like interruptions initiating openness and wonder, a suspension of that pattern is necessary to appreciate and extricate from it. His whole life long Malcolm X consistently separated from the patterns of hypocrisy, and he called all of us to do the same, to separate ourselves from our deceptive propensities in order to embody our receptive ones. Conditioned by this "reinvention," Malcolm X lived a tragically short but honest life, a life shaped by wonder, openness, and receptivity. Malcolm X stands out in the history of this epoch as a magnanimous man, a great American.[12] Details of his biography will offer clear signals of what it means to be a receptive person who pursues the moral and political implications of what has been learned.

RECEPTIVITY EXEMPLIFIED: MALCOLM X

One may wonder why Malcolm X would be an exemplar in receptivity. Wasn't he outspoken and virulent in his opposition to the white power structure, uncompromising in his scathing critique of other civil rights leaders who, to his mind, acquiesced to white governmental and religious leaders? He did not seem to be dialogical in his teaching. Wasn't he unabashedly a black nationalist, unreceptive to the idea that blacks and whites should work together for justice? I want to suggest that indeed, he was uncompromising, outspoken, and unabashed. But these adjectives can readily be applied to his encounter with, and articulation of, truth. Receptivity as engrossment is the intellectual endurance necessary to see the implications of truth, and, to apply that learning to one's existence, especially when it comes between one's most valued and loyal relationships. Unlike so many of us who measure truth by way of our loyalties and relationships, Malcolm X consistently measured his relationships by truth, and that made all the difference.[13]

12. I am conscious of this being a contentious statement. And I am aware that it may even be offensive to some who see that designation as a betrayal of Malcolm X's teaching and legacy. But, when "we" claim this person as a product of this continent, and we don't water down his critique, we can identify ourselves as a people of critical and constructive reason.

13. Aristotle proposed that the mark of a philosopher is the persistent tendency to pursue truth, even at the expense of friendship, the loyalty between teacher and student. He mentions this in his *Nicomachean Ethics*, 9, as he explains the disagreement he has

RECEIVING AND PERCEIVING

When Malcolm Little was four years old, his house burned to the ground; he looked on while it blazed. Two years later, his father, a local black leader, was found dead on the railroad tracks in Lansing, Michigan. Malcolm's mother tried to hold the family together, but as Malcolm came into adolescence, his mother was sent to an asylum. Malcolm was then sent to a detention home run by a nice white couple, Mr. and Mrs. Swerlin. His older sister, born of his father's first marriage, lived in Boston. Malcolm visited Boston and saw there a black culture unlike the fragmented one in Michigan. He later moved to Boston and became active in the social scene, especially the street scene, where he learned how to survive and thrive. He was arrested for armed robbery in 1946. While in prison, he encountered the teachings of the honorable Elijah Mohammed and converted to the Nation of Islam in 1948–49.[14] From 1954 until he left the Nation in 1964, he became the most revered teacher in the Nation of Islam. He traveled the world in his ministry of empowerment and teaching. He confronted the honorable Elijah Mohammed when he learned of rumors of his adultery, since it was discovered that the leader had fathered children with his young secretaries. He was silenced by Elijah Mohammed in 1963 for public comments he had made regarding the assassination of President John F. Kennedy. He left the Nation of Islam in 1964. He then went to Mecca, where he was a pilgrim on the Hajj, a required ritual for Muslims and one of the five pillars of Islam, thus confirming unequivocally his break from the sectarian Nation of Islam, and his embrace of universal Islamic brotherhood. He also visited the African continent and learned about their unified political structure, which he then sought to implement in the United States, which he did in 1964, forming *The Organization of Afro-American Unity*. At that point, his teaching took on a more universal, but no less prophetic turn. He was assassinated as he spoke at one of those meetings, February 21, 1965.[15]

---

with his teacher Plato's conception of the good as an abstract form. Malcolm X's disagreement with Elijah Mohammed grew out of his discovery of the sad truth of his teacher's adultery, which amounted to preying on and impregnating his secretaries, teenage girls. See X, *Autobiography*, 339–43.

14. Malcolm X, *Autobiography*, 5–6, 13, 42, 30.

15. Malcolm X, *Autobiography*, 338–47, 432, 441–78.

MALCOLM X: EXPERIENCES OF THINKING, THINKING ABOUT EXPERIENCES

We see receptivity in Malcolm X's childhood experience. Two examples I would like to point out. First, in his experience in the detention home, his presence and social gregariousness was positively received by the nice white couple, the Swerlins. He recollects their interest in his abilities, his work-ethic, and how he got along with the other children. But in the same breath, he remembers, the Swerlins would talk about him and other black people as if Malcolm was not in the room.[16] In talking with a teacher he had been receptive to, one Mr. Ostrowski, Malcolm Little was asked what he wanted to do when he grew up. He quickly answered, "I'd like to be a lawyer." He admits that he had not thought at all about a career, but his eagerness to reciprocate Mr. Ostrowski's receptivity of Malcolm may have prompted him to say something he thought the teacher would appreciate hearing. Mr. Ostrowski then told Malcolm Little to be "realistic," and that being a lawyer in Lansing, MI was just not realistic for a person like Malcolm, a black person. Here we see an encounter of mutual receptivity between teacher and student that is skewed by institutional and social prejudices. Malcolm X received the goodness of the presence of Mr. Ostrowski, but he was given ideas that never did square with Malcolm Little's probing intelligence. Ostrowski received the student's existence from a frame of reference destructive of the very craft he dedicated his life to, teaching. To clarify the fact that racism and the white-superiority complex is institutionalized, socialized, and perpetuated throughout U.S. culture, Malcolm X prefaces his description of this encounter, saying: "I know he probably meant well in what he happened to advise me that day. I doubt that he meant any harm. It was just in his nature as an American white man." According to Malcolm X, the nature of every white man is to have this frame of reference skewed by the institutional patterns of history, premised of course on the pattern of slavery. Every teacher, including me, has brought relational prejudices into the classroom with them, which impact the learning environment. Appreciating that encounter of Malcolm X, we can infer how many dissociative experiences of receptivity cloud young minds with doubt, insecurity, and shame. And then we can consider the tremendous negative impact of institutional practices and habits which impinge upon the souls of diverse populations of students. Despite good intentions, we are still prone

16. Malcolm X, *Autobiography*, 32.

to prejudices *unless* we can develop the capacity for engrossment, a non-selective presence of reception of every student's fragile reason.

In thinking about his experience, that encounter was given context and deeper meaning after he went to Boston to visit his older sister. There, he was receptive to a new social reality, the encounter with a black culture that was more autonomous, self-enclosed, and flourishing. There he saw black lawyers, black teachers, black-owned businesses. When he returned to the detention home, he understood Mr. Ostrowski's reception of him in a whole new light, a new frame of reference. He suggests too that they noticed the change in him, and he no longer would act like their "mascot." This autobiographical account of Malcolm X's dynamic receptivity gives us a glimpse into an intelligence at work connecting patterns and forging novel understandings consistent with facts. But it also demonstrates how intransigent are the white power structure's premises. They remain embedded in consciousness until we practice "the non-selective presence" called for by Nel Noddings' ethical ideal. In Malcolm X, see how receptivity is an exponential experience, involving time, memory, renewal of mind, and emotional maturity in a dynamic encounter with thinking, others, and ideas.

RECEIVING TRUTH INTERRUPTS THE RELATIONAL PATTERN

Certainly, being in prison in the late 1940s conditioned the prisoner's reason. By his own account, Malcolm X's prison experience radically transformed his identity. He became receptive to his siblings who wrote letters to him about a new faith they had become a part of, the Nation of Islam. That intrigued him, and for the first time, he got down on his knees and prayed. That action, receptivity in its kinesthetic structure, promoted a new frame of reference through which he saw his whole experience and the country in which he lived. It was a novel, liberating construct. Good and evil had become located in light of Allah's favor; the white man was the devil. Yet in affirming that idea, Malcolm X simultaneously acknowledged his own evil, and sought to surrender to Allah, what he called "the hardest thing in the world." So, before we critique the view of white people given by Elijah Mohammed,[17] let us move into Malcolm Little's frame of refer-

---

17. Interestingly, in philosophical terms, this dichotomous thinking is known as the *black-and-white fallacy*. This fallacy is entrenched most clearly in the Republican/

ence. He is in jail, his mother was in a mental institution at the hands of a paternalistic social welfare system, and his father was left to be cut up on the railroad tracks outside of town, the perpetrators never prosecuted.[18] He was the mascot of a detention home, and so forth. When he experiences his thinking while thinking about his experience, that dualistic metaphysical construct opened a new possibility, a new Malcolm. His anger no longer infused his prideful criminality (a construct activated by white power structures), but in his prayer that pride dissipated, as he received the pride of his native identity, African identity. In that intellectual conversion, Malcolm X gave his assent to the Honorable Elijah Mohammed, the "prophet" who developed the mythological horizon and the vision for infrastructure of the Nation of Islam. Malcolm X would become a leader among the men of the organization, the Fruit of Islam, and in that role, he would actualize his tremendous gifts, and his incisive social analysis. But, Malcolm X's fertile mind, which deconstructed not only America's superiority complex but also was able to convey clearly a global movement of solidarity, went well beyond the teaching of Elijah Mohammed. That teaching, propelled by truth, would lead Malcolm X to eventually deconstruct his loyalty to the Nation of Islam, in his ongoing intellectual and spiritual conversion in truth.

READING AND RECEIVING THE TIME

Prior to being arrested, Malcolm X was the ring-leader of a poorly organized, amateur criminal organization, a gang that would rob homes in suburban Boston. Malcolm X was at fault for them getting caught, since he was loose with gifts to his family and selling to jewelers meant that police could trace the "hot" items back to the gang. When Malcolm X was arrested, the police promised him a lighter sentence if he would rat out his fellow gang members; he did, and of course the police did not make good on their promise—although they did for the white girl who was part of the gang. She only served seven months of a five-year sentence.[19] When he first

---

Democratic dichotomy in the U.S. That presumption, and its confirmation in memes, news, and journalistic vengefulness, is successful in turning any intelligent person away from politics; and that may be its very purpose, just ask those paid millions to be political consultants.

18. Marable Manning, *Malcolm X*, 30–32.
19. Marable Manning, *Malcolm X*, 68–69.

arrived in Boston five years earlier, he familiarized himself with the region by "roaming," walking to the campuses surrounding the city. He would ride the subway to the end of the line. One day he got off at Cambridge and he

> Circled all around in the Harvard University campus. Somewhere, I had already heard of Harvard—though I didn't know much more about it. Nobody that day could have told me I would give an address before the Harvard Law School Forum some twenty years later.[20]

We hear of wonder here, being happily perplexed, able to encounter Harvard again in a novel frame of reference. When any of us are consistently receptive to new frames of reference we do get that sense of wonder at how we came to this time, this place. Malcolm X's wonder as he shares his memories of Harvard ("nobody could have told me") evinces that sense of surrender implicit in receptivity, when we are open enough, given over to the truth of historical contingencies. Part of that contingency is a receptivity of our own limits, in knowledge, in goodness. Malcolm X reflects on this existential vulnerability, as he thinks about his prison experience:

> I have since learned—helping me to understand what then began to happen within me—that the truth can be quickly received, or received at all, only by the sinner who knows and admits that he is guilty of having sinned much. Stated another way: only guilt admitted accepts truth.[21]

Is not his insight the reason that he understood so well northern white liberals'[22] hypocrisy? Malcolm X's penetrating analysis of the white power structure persistently exposed this inability of whites to actively pursue this kind of receptive surrender to the facts of American history. Whites are stuck in this pattern of ignorant optimism, an ignorance that Aristotle has described as a chosen ignorance; and, according to the *Nicomachean Ethics*, when we choose not to know something, we are not exonerated from

---

20. Malcolm X, *Autobiography*, 50.

21. Malcolm X, *Autobiography*, 189.

22. Malcolm X's unsparing critique of the hypocrisy of the northern white liberals gets to the very heart of the U.S.'s moral problem, power and privilege cocooned from encountering the brutal realities of existence all the while feigning "care" about matters considered irrelevant to life in their cocoon. Today, the idiom *white people's problems* is at once coy and disgraceful. But it expresses well the shallow and insular experience of white privilege. See Malcolm X, *Autobiography*, 312, for a scathing critique. For an extended discussion of such white insulation, see DiAngelo, *White Fragility*, 55.

blame.[23] Borgmann's analysis of the device pattern and commodification is not all that different. For that ubiquitous pattern consistently sets up a process through which we are divorced from the truth of our condition. Racism and commodification are initiated most graphically in American slavery. The device paradigm is the distant cousin of the slave economy.

RECEPTION: WORD AND WILL

His prison experience, according to Malcolm X, made him "the closest thing to a hermit." And, he says,

> I still marvel at how swiftly my previous life's thinking pattern slid away from me, like snow off a roof. It is as though someone else I knew of had lived by hustling and crime. I would be startled to catch myself thinking in a remote way of my earlier self as another person.[24]

Like Merton, Malcolm X entered a disciplined and studied existence, one of focus, silence, prayer, transformation. This self-education, separated and so uniquely different from his peers' "white" educations (think Martin Luther King, Jr.) provided for Malcolm X an intransigent capacity to understand the truth through deep social analysis, and would lead him to the global stage, beyond the provincialities of American thought and myopia. He understood that myopia through his study of the English language. The effective communicator is never grandiose, and communication is effected only to the degree that the truth of concrete realities may be appreciated. How did he learn so deeply about the hypocrisy of white culture? He copied every entry of the English dictionary, A-Z. It led to this intellectual confidence: "I could for the first time pick up a book and read and now begin to understand what the book was saying. Anyone who has read a great deal can imagine the new world that opened."[25] The fundamental substrate of every other pattern is some form of language, be it programming a computer, tweeting, or conversing. Reading and copying the dictionary would give Malcolm X a nimble intellect and avail him of critique, no matter the object. The arduous copying task, like a monk's transcribing biblical texts,

23. The discussion is in Aristotle's Book 3, chapter 5, of the *Nicomachean Ethics*, 52. Aristotle calls this kind of ignorance "*careless* ignorance."

24. Malcolm X, *Autobiography*, 196.

25. Malcolm X, *Autobiography*, 199.

embeds a fundamental integrative focus for all subsequent reading and speaking. Simply look up any one of Malcolm X's speeches or interviews, and you will hear someone who presents to us modernity's apex of literacy. But that literacy was not applied to some specialized academic daydream, aloof from concrete realities. Malcolm X's specialty, the command of the language, was leveraged to find the particulars of the truth, eventually opening up the global scope on race relations. Along with his receptivity, his intelligence and his work ethic, this alternative education, it seems, outperformed his interlocutors, who rarely had the same respect or passion for truth, a truth that tends to come between us and our most cherished loyalties.

Leaving the Nation of Islam set Malcolm X free in one sense, but also placed upon his shoulders the responsibility for a new movement in unity among African peoples in the United States. This vision was provoked by two significant events: his trip to Mecca, participating in the pilgrimage with worldwide ordinary Muslims, known as Hajj, and his engagement with African leaders who had been successful in their revolutionary activity to throw off colonialist oppressors. Receptive to both African solidarity and a universal experience of brotherhood, notably including whites, promoted a dynamic new pattern of thought that was described by Malcolm X as an expansion of his "scope." To many in the American scene, black and white, this receptivity upset the racial norms that had propelled Malcolm X to prominence. Certainly, the Nation of Islam, a sectarian organization, would deem him a heretic. But other black separatists wondered if this Islamic vision of brotherhood undercut the power of his analysis of white racism.[26]

MALCOLM X: DISTINCTION IN RECEPTIVITY

Receptivity to truth means that we hold together what E. F. Schumacher has called divergent ideas. In the case of American racism, binary, easy, and untenable are the solutions to either separate or integrate. Oft-times, ideas may converge, as when faith and reason are complementary modes of discovery. But in the modern period, the great increase in varying scientific methods, the refinement of contradictory conclusions into dichotomous convictions, has led to the proliferation of divergent solutions. Schumacher cites the

---

26. For descriptions of this widening scope, see Malcolm X, *Autobiography*, 416; for a description of how this broadening affected his diverse audiences back in the States, see Marable Manning, *Malcolm X*, 328.

divergent ideas of the purposes of education, a relevant inquiry here, as an example: is the purpose of education to instill discipline and obedience or foster freedom?[27] Today, is the purpose of education career readiness or cultural appropriation—say, the culture of democracy? We can bridge those dichotomies by making distinctions. There are some subjects within curricular structures that never lend themselves to utilitarian purposes, the study of history, for example. Those same subjects must temper the strictly utilitarian competencies that tend to detach us from more formative intellectual processes, like reading a novel or studying an historical figure like John Brown. Easy answers generally take form as our imaginations and experience become insular; thus we live and act upon those dichotomies without considering distinctions. The reprehensible commercial form of this unreceptive human tendency is that disjunction between Fox News and CNN. The corporations that bait a numb populace with easy answers rooted in fear and anger, have seriously weakened the intellectual weight of the United States citizenry. How do we hold together the awful truth of white privilege, a solution being separation and segregation, and the teaching of universal human brotherhood/sisterhood, a staple of every major religion? Malcolm X's receptivity is a lesson for all of us. When receptive to the truth, we must be ready to make careful distinctions while leaving the comfort of our thin divergences. With Malcolm X, we must take the time to acknowledge, communicate, and clarify the meaning of those distinctions. Upon his return from the Middle East, more than once Malcolm X made distinctions about whites in America that enabled him to corroborate the American reality. This renewed vision, we must make clear, was due primarily to the Hajj, the pilgrimage that brings the world to Mecca. In his travel diary, Malcolm X would write about the Hajj:

> Everyone forgets Self and turns to God and out of this submission to the One God comes a brotherhood in which all are equals. . . . [T]here is no greater serenity of mind . . . than when one can shut out the hectic noise and pace of the materialistic outside world, and seek inner peace within oneself. . . . The very essence of Islam religion in teaching the Oneness of God, gives the Believer genuine, voluntary obligations towards his fellow man (all of whom are One Human Family, brothers and sisters to each other)[;] . . . the True Believer recognizes the Oneness of all Humanity.[28]

27. Schumacher, *A Guide for the Perplexed*, 120–23.
28. As quoted in Marable Manning, *Malcolm X*, 311.

Here we have further evidence of the kinesthetic aspect of receptivity, a conscious practice of surrender. That sacred experience imbued his vision to include white people as part of the solution, not merely as part of the problem. This vision is given concrete expression in a speech Malcolm X gave at Corn Hill Methodist Church in Rochester, New York, five days before his assassination. A lesson on globalization and colonialism, a clear and distinct teaching on white privilege, and, with great foresight, an analysis of the role of the white-owned media in propagating the image of African Americans as criminals, make this speech especially relevant for us. But he begins, interestingly, by inviting his audience into receptivity. Malcolm X was funny, and humor was at times a rhetorical strategy. In the '50s, Corn Hill Methodist attempted to forge an inter-racial church. There were whites in the audience and Malcolm X invited all to enter receptively this environment.

> One of the reasons I feel that it is best to remain very informal when discussing this type of topic, when people are discussing things based on race, they have a tendency to be very narrow-minded and to get emotional and all involved in—especially white people. I have found white people that usually are very intelligent, until you get them to talking about the race problem. Then they get blind as a bat and want you to see what they know is the exact opposite of the truth. [Applause] So what I would rather try and do is be very informal, where we can relax and keep an open mind, and try and form the pattern of the habit of seeing for ourselves, hearing for ourselves, thinking for ourselves, and then we can come to an intelligent judgment for ourselves.[29]

Receptivity is the encounter that evokes in us intellectual self-trust in what we hear, in what we think, and in our capacity for judgment. Malcolm X then places before his audience a category of understanding that is able to hold together the tension between his earlier appropriation of American white racism, understanding that all white people were somehow infected with this evil, and his new appropriation of Islamic universalism, that the "brotherhood of man" is true. Speaking of Jesus, Moses, and Muhammad in an effort to clarify the dignity of humanity, Malcolm X affirms his new position by invoking the category of *practice*.

> I believe in the brotherhood of man. But despite the fact that I believe in the brotherhood of man, I have to be a realist and realize

29. Malcolm X, *The Last Speeches*, 156.

that here in America we're in a society that doesn't practice brotherhood. It doesn't practice what it preaches. It preaches brotherhood, but doesn't practice brotherhood.[30]

How do we practice our political and religious convictions? How do
we practice a belief in the direct effects of consumerism on the warming
of the oceans, and practice this belief? Practice, that is, concrete embodied
acts, is the measurement of our knowledge and moral claims. Malcolm X
did not mean, however, that no whites practiced brotherhood. Never letting
anyone off the hook, Malcolm X continues by making distinctions in order
to drive home his point. In the U.S., those with the power have traditionally
maintained that power by way of separating people.

> We are living in a society that is by and large controlled by people
> who believe in segregation. We are living in a society that is by and
> large controlled by a people who believe in racism. And I say it is
> controlled, not by well-meaning whites, but controlled . . . by the
> racists.[31]

An implication of his analysis is that we "well-meaning people" are
not a factor within the power structure's active engagement in maintaining
that power. This power, according to Malcolm X, controls public opinion
and this message "is a very skillful message used by racists to make the
whites who aren't racists think that the rate of crime in the Black community is so high. This keeps the black community in the image of the
criminal."[32] Millions of dollars are spent on acquiring this skill, a college
major called "marketing." And many more billions are spent paying people
for this skill. Today we swim so deeply through propaganda and marketing campaigns and strategies that we may fail to be receptive to this 1965
analysis by Malcolm X:

> This is a skill. This skill is called—this is a science that's called "im-
> age making." They hold you in check through this science of imag-
> ery. They even make you look down upon yourself, by giving you
> a bad image of yourself. Some of our own Black people who have
> eaten this image themselves and digested it—until they themselves
> don't want to live in the Black community. They don't want to be
> around Black people themselves. [Applause][33]

30. Malcolm X, *The Last Speeches*, 157.
31. Malcolm X, *Malcolm X Speaks*, 158.
32. Malcolm X, *Malcolm X Speaks*, 160.
33. Malcolm X, *The Last Speeches*, 160.

This insight into journalism is a premonition of our contemporary quotidian barrage of images which confine the minds of the well-meaning. Sometimes, the truth is mediated; oftentimes it is drowned in a sea of distraction. Through Malcolm X's receptivity to truth, we can glean the following precepts from his teaching. All our learning takes place in a particular ecology, whether it be the humanistic ecology of the Hajj or the hyper-reality of contemporary media ecology. Each ecology will infuse our learning and practice within certain parameters, structures of routine. Encounters that are open carriers of wonder are often those that are undergone in novel environments. And when receptive to truth, we may measure the less humane and authentic encounter by the more. Receptivity, as has been shown all along, yields a deeply qualitative perceptual grasp. Becoming receptive to others and to ideas eventually yields a more realistic discernment of ourselves, both our limits and our gifts. When Malcolm X invited his audience to relax and enter a more informal environment, he was priming the listener's pump. Listening is a skill that propagandists understand and manipulate in their technocratic branding. To apply and refine our receptive capacities, we must reflect on the lost art of listening.

RECEPTIVITY APPLIED: LISTENING

"Multiphrenia is a consciousness structured by a variety of value systems born in conflicting cultural worlds. Its effects are many. It means being subject to the demands of a variety of groups, torn between obligations and even between realities. And with that comes an enduring sense of inadequacy, failure, and high anxiety. One's sense of reality, truth, reasonableness is compromised to the degree that these things are splintered among the many worlds that take residence in consciousness."

—Edward Farley

These words of Edward Farley were written as the millennials were coming into this world. Farley's sense then was that institutions vie for loyalty and even religion becomes beholden to its own survival, so much so that the sphere of the inter-human is largely ignored in our broader culture. For Farley, "inter-human" refers to Martin Buber's description of human encounter. It is that encounter through which another sphere opens up, and we become less dependent on autonomous projects of becoming "oneself" and more open to discovery of meaning and purpose beyond each institutional loyalty. In the inter-human we find ourselves unfettered from the familial, institutional, branded identities that keep us satisfied with surface issues of pleasure in consumption. The inter-human is the Hajj, but also the speech at Cornhill Methodist church in Rochester, NY. In the twenty-first century where do we find the inter-human conserved and expanded? Our religious communities? But how do children teach us, and how do we model for them, that life is more than the mesmerizing smart phone without which they become anxious? And how might we foster engrossment, the basis of which is the virtue of listening, in this era of amplified Multiphrenia? Education has to be the place of conservation.

Each encounter in thought has its corresponding practice, which gives each of us concrete application in our learning. Practicing brotherhood, as Malcolm X puts it, demands listening. Our capacity to listen is directly proportional to our self-knowledge, the genuine fluency of our inner dialogue. It is because we are fluent with the distinctiveness of our inner conversation that we can recognize the uniqueness of another, and listen attentively and at first non-selectively in order to allow that person to manifest what they themselves have been asking, as it were, in their own heads. To be a good listener, we have to appreciate "the many worlds that take residence in our heads," and learn to judge and release those voices that fail to comply with the truth. This is hard work. But having worked through this inner prognostication, we can more aptly set it aside, in order to hear another into speech. In touch with our unique inner dialogue, we then confront a basic inter-personal principle: each person is distinct and different.

CULTIVATION: A CULTURE OF LISTENING

Because most of us can hear, and the "best and the brightest" are expected to do the most talking, listening, a sign of consistent moral awareness, is under-served. But good listeners become bright, clear-headed, and keen because of the work they have put into listening. The capacity to listen has to be honed and refined. The discipline required to become a good listener can be applied in other aspects of life and work. What kind of discipline is listening?

First, in order to listen well, we have to decide that listening is hard work. Malcolm X asked people (white people) to relax in order to open themselves. However, once that invitation goes forth, it is up to the listener to resist their ego to enter the life-world of another. Listening is the inverse of our tendency to complain at the slightest challenge to our needs and perceptions. It requires a suspension of our selfishness while simultaneously offering oneself to become engrossed in that which is said, in word, gesture, tone, and so forth.

Secondly, we really have to decide to tune out our own ideas, our need for acknowledgement, our desire for attention, but most of all, our presumptions of knowledge. Listening, if you will, is the teleological suspension of the personal. The purpose is to receptively enter the inter-personal, in order to learn: to hear someone into speech, to appreciate their insight, to adjudicate and parse the truth of the matter, which now exists somewhere between. That between is *the place* truth has always been, and by listening we enter genuinely into that presence.

Third, the emotions must be governed during listening. This takes the most practice, and perhaps is the most compromised dimension of listening in a digital age. Governing the emotions does not mean that they are ignored as a Stoic would ignore them. It means, rather, that pathos (passion) is most useful when tempered and "cut" by reason, releasing the curiosity necessary to attune to that which is being listened to. Because curiosity has an emotional substrate, those energies need to be channeled into that inquisitive disposition that is listening.

Fourth, listening carries itself differently into different contexts of learning. We learn that we must first "listen" to the context through which our listening will be offered. I listen to a hematology lecture differently than I listen to a teammate, especially if I am squeamish. I listen to a friend's story of his/her break-up differently than I listen to a podcast on romantic relationships. I govern my anxiety when listening to the latest updates on the tax code, especially if my experiences as a tax-payer have been fraught with ambiguity and distrust. In this fourth aspect, however, there is the opportunity for novelty. This is so because I can only partially read and listen to the context of my listening prior to the actual listening. If I decide prior to entering the context what I will feel like, what will happen, then I come into a new listening environment already fettered to my mind's structure of prejudices. I think I know the pattern and fail to cultivate openness and wonder as the conditions of my learning, the conditions which tend not to place prior conditions on what I will be listening for or to. Yet another vital condition of this fourth aspect is to draw strategies for listening that turn back those structural prejudices. This is how receptive listening is forever broadening its scope of learning. In listening well, the scope of our conversation broadens, and we become more and more particular. Put another way, our significance seems to diminish as the scope of what is real widens. Genuine listening can put us in touch with our finitude. This existential fact is amplified when infused with our next discussion, the meaning and measure of contemplation in a frenetic, digital age.

5

Contemplation

THE CONTEXT OF OUR CONTEMPLATIVE PROSPECT

THOMAS MERTON'S LAST DAYS were spent in conversation; he had been teaching about, and listening for, the renewal of monastic life and its global/inter-religious impact. Merton and others like him were both aware and attendant to the emptiness of technocratic society, of management, efficiency, marketing, and even social engineering. Monastics like Merton, enveloped by solitude, felt deeply the sorrow of mass culture and the pervasive insecurity and anxiety that surfaced as the twentieth century grew ever dimmer. In that way his witness is consistent—his lifestyle and writing/testimony are one whole thing; a matter of health, edification, and invitation. The question is, to what did he invite us?[1]

We can get into this question by considering the following fact: Merton's degree of solitude had a proportionate effect on his pastoral insight and love for humanity. His detachment attached him, through love, to a hurting world. It is the practice of intentional detachment that attaches our minds and hearts to significance. For Eva Saulitis, it was a detachment

---

1. The foregoing will describe contemplation within the context of contemporary existence. For more extensive appreciation I suggest Thomas Merton, *New Seeds of Contemplation*, especially chapter 2, titled, "Solitude Is Not Separation," 52–63. For a more recent attempt to articulate the significance of contemplative prayer, see, Keating, *Open Mind Open Heart*.

from the expectations of success in the 1980s, then a detachment from a conventional career. This detachment attached her mind and heart to a love of cetaceans, a love of ecological replete-ness, and an awareness of the public-health dangers of post-industrial culture. And, for Malcolm X, a consistent detachment from lies and falsehoods, from hypocrisy, enabled him to simultaneously deconstruct and teach about the violence inherent in white power and privilege. Also, this sort of detachment attached him ultimately to a universal truth, the potential of religious consciousness to free humanity for cooperation.

These ways of detachment are motivated by a moral sense; there is an "ought" aspect in detachment that motivates us to let go of falsity, contempt, insecurity, and the frivolous. In this encounter of thought, an encounter with our innate moral depth, we are no longer bound to the expectations and values of a status quo, even if that status has a degree of positive ef-fect. This sort of detachment ultimately leads to free thought, as we attach assertively to the weight of our moral, intellectual, and spiritual power. It is a detachment by which other encounters, in thought and deed, can be weighed, as long as we continue to move within that order of the mind, an order that our cognitive and emotive syntax is inclined to actively pursue. That search for the ordering of the mind, a way of thinking with the grain of ultimate meanings and purposes, is active in the child, the adolescent, the adult, all of us. This is why children ask such great questions, why students are enlivened by silence and nature, why adults are restless in their busyness.

That adult busyness may have something to do with the patterns that groove our expectations. Borgmann's analysis demonstrates that the device paradigm has a kind of detachment as well. This is a detachment from en-counter itself, the encounter with others, machinery, complexity, nature, place. A detachment from those focal practices that would cauterize and capitalize ultimate meanings. This detachment, a process of disburdenment that feeds the habit of expecting convenience and efficiency, presents itself as a way to order our minds, our relationships, our consumptions. This detachment in disburdenment entails an attachment too, an attachment to convenience and distraction. And thus, this detachment is a simulacrum of the detachment that attaches us to ultimacy. It is a surface and superficial condition of pursuing magic and ease, giving us the sense that we have actualized some meaningful value. Think of cell phone use in particular. In a habitual, say, religious sort of way, persons carve space and time to scroll, game, text. To see themselves afresh through media that is social. It is a self-imposed detachment in order to garner some sense of self. Contemplation, a gaze of the mind enticing our very best thoughts, lifts the veil on magic and ease to enter wonder and grace. This too is a detachment, except that the encounter is not social and frenetic. Contemplation is learned when we cease to be captive to the murmurings of social toil, and permit Another to gently redirect the mind's spasms. Time is the indispensable partner in this renewal in detachment. The urgent detachment of the device paradigm works parasitically on our longing to contemplate ultimate matters, to order our minds to the most significant goods of the soul, of life. If we are to appreciate contemplation in an age like ours, we ought to analyze the detachment/attachment dynamic at work in the patterns of contemporary existence, and the order of the human mind.

RELIEVING AND PERCEIVING

The detachment of the device paradigm confirms two values of contemporary experience, convenience and diversion. Reaching out a hand can disencumber, or disburden, a friend struggling to carry three suitcases at a time. When done, relief is the feeling the friend has and gratitude is the result. In the inter-personal encounter of disburdenment there is one who disburdens and one who is disburdened. It is pretty clear that as an action, disburdenment is a good; it is also clear that such action has a positive result on the carrier of the burden, unless pride gets the best of that person and they refuse the offer of disburdenment. Inversely, there are those who get carried away, having a hero's complex; they work very hard at relieving all manner of persons from ostensible stress and strain. Unless they are told otherwise, they become attuned to apparent need in all circumstances and prevail upon others their special "burden" of helping at every turn. In this way, those accustomed, even addicted, to disburdening others fail to perceive in others or themselves *the good of human struggle*. The encounter of disburdenment between people can help us to appreciate how technological disburdenment mimics the best of our intentions. But this replication serves mostly to attach us to the presumption of the device pattern. We thus miss the extent to which personal struggle is necessary for intellectual and spiritual growth.

Trusting in the Good of Struggle

For example, take an encounter between two persons. An elderly person who desires to walk by himself to the grocery store, for the primary reason of exercise, is someone who feels burdened by the offers to make his experience *easier*. Disburdenment can be good in the interpersonal sphere, but clearly, struggle has a role in the development of human good, or virtue. If attempting to maintain balance and stamina, the last thing that person may want is a ride, which would only circumvent his plan to keep on walking.

If one did not know the walker personally, and yet saw him on the way to the suburban grocery four blocks from his house, one might feel the strain of perplexity that a person of that age would be walking the street. If one is at all socially adept, questions might arise: Doesn't that person have a car? Was his license stripped? Doesn't he have a family to drive him somewhere? Perplexity might recede to pity, mild scorn, and perhaps a shaking of the head. Yet if you asked the walker, he could say: "I need the exercise, and the grocery store has local vegetables that I know came in today. I want to cook fresh vegetables this evening for my grandchildren." That answer, though reasonable, may nevertheless result in, "Well, you should really get a ride, be safe; there is no reason you need to walk." For those who have been socialized to favor the values of convenience and efficiency, the burden of walking as a good does not register. And why would walking be a good? Especially for those who get in their cars in their garages, open the door with a button, drive in air-conditioning twenty minutes to work, park in a downtown parking garage, walk indoors to their offices, eat lunch in the building's basement restaurant, finish work, get in their car, drive, open the garage door, park, take off their shoes, and watch the evening news, which includes ominous weather reports, crime, scandal, and all manner of commercials telling them how much they deserve every comfort, convenience, elegance, and euphoria at practically no cost to them. The sweat on the brow of the elderly walker is an affront to those who conform consistently to the culture of technology, a culture that prides itself on the ostensible good of all manner of disburdenment. But this detachment from burdens also, we notice, detaches us from perceiving correctly *the good* our elder walker desires. We see then, that disburdenment in contemporary terms is a bit more complex than the good of relieving someone of their burden. It is understood practically through the technological pattern, a pattern that has culminated in a distorted correspondence between our ideas of struggle and the actuality or purpose of that same struggle. This is especially the case in terms of boredom, so called "downtime," or the simple fact of having nothing to do. We might call this the struggle of solitude. When bored, with nothing to do, we encounter our mind's multi-frenetic aimlessness. But when we intend to face our boredom with the aim of considering ultimate matters, boredom can be transformed into contemplation. For that is something of what contemplation is: The slow entrance into a more unified moment of awareness resulting in a focus on ultimacy.

PATTERN AND ORDER

To this point in the discussion, "pattern" has been considered in two related ways:

A. Relational patterns of knowing—with others, nature, truth, experience.

B. Patterns of culture, e.g., the technological or device pattern, those patterns that have been confirmed and more firmly instantiated through the values that result from, and drive, the technological culture: efficiency, convenience, and commodification.

As these patterns have been described, it is apparent that B tends to weaken A. And this has all sorts of moral implications that are intricately linked to teaching, learning, nature, and culture. What is in order, then, as we think about the nature of contemplation, is a more abstract consideration of what a pattern is. Thus, we distinguish between a *pattern* and an *order*. The order of our minds can then critique and transform the patterns that impact us. This is another way of discussing the relation between theory and practice, or in religious terms, contemplation and action. It is synergy. Theory and practice: always perceiving, receiving, and acting; contemplation and action, receptive, perceptive, and active. The mind's order, like theory and contemplation, impacts the way we approach life's habits and patterns. The ordering of our minds is the work of contemplation; the transfiguration of the pattern then can follow pretty close behind. However, it is probably not very helpful to put this synergy in dialectical terms, since that would serve only to narrow the mystery we discuss here, making it into some sort of model or program, which it can never become.

PATTERN AND UTILITY

Patterns are designs, and we designate things by way of their patterns. Geese fly so high, and at that height are arranged in a V formation, leveraging physical atmospheric processes for their corporate flight. Patterns of traffic are established through work-schedules, highway utilities, and speed limits. Artwork has patterns; comedy is designed for tension and catharsis; visual art plays with pattern and variability; both jazz and classical music take up patterned themes and work them through, amplifying them now, reintroducing the pattern more subtly then. There are patterns of consumption: of natural resources, food, pharmaceuticals, alcohol, tobacco; these patterns are set very often in the corporate boardrooms of global capitalism, or sometimes regulations are invoked to slow, or correct a pattern that has proven itself over-reaching or downright dangerous. All these patterns have something they acquire and accomplish. Geese fly longer and stronger in their pattern. Traffic patterns ensure that accidents are kept to a minimum and quick access to places of employment is ensured. Art elevates the human spirit and helps us to recognize both the misery and glory of human existence. Consumption is necessary for living, and infrastructure and supply chains ensure that people have access to commodities. Patterns are good, but they are not *interminable*. Our minds, however, become accustomed and attached to certain patterns, and the expectations and benefits from these patterns take hold of our imaginations, making us myopic.

The pattern can dictate our moments to such a degree that alternatives seem irrational. At that point our minds are ordered to the pattern, rather than the order of our minds seeing pattern for what it is, as *just* a pattern. When the order of the mind sees through the pattern, we can say, "It doesn't have to be that way." Unless you are a goose, of course. Patterns generally mediate a purpose; a utility and the value of utility is inscribed within the pattern.

CONTEMPLATION: DESCRIPTION

But order implies not only utility, but also a way of prioritization based upon qualitative criteria. These criteria move well beyond cost-benefit analysis, convenience and utility. An order, and mindful ordering, assembles moral and aesthetic reason. Order is both a verb and a noun. When I order at a restaurant, I am making judgments based on criteria in the moment. For example, I may have had seafood at the restaurant before, but just read a study on the depletion of the tuna population in the Atlantic Ocean, so that may affect my thinking as I order and the order may reflect this new appreciation. Order is a noun. The order then becomes a possessive, it is mine. The waiter may wonder, "Did he order salad or bread with his meal? I'll have to ask him about *his* order." Ordering is driven by broad considerations involving adjudicatory capacities and we take care at restaurants because our ordering is the foresight of our qualitative experience, the very way we experience the pattern of dining. The order could radically change the dining pattern. Analogously, the order of our minds can result in analyzing its own patterns of thought and freely detaching from the patterns.

In the restaurant, sometimes those criteria for ordering could be based on things to avoid, foods and drinks that compromise the patterns of tastes I have developed over the years. In this case, the criteria are something like: I make my order based upon what I *don't* want and what will *not* upset some perceived equilibria in my diet and metabolism. Rather than ordering based on what is good, we order based on *avoiding* what is bad. These are two very different methods of ordering the mind. Looking for the good, we anticipate, we imagine, we adjudicate our past in relation to the future. Looking to avoid what is bad, we narrow our scope, we recollect prior bad experiences, we control. We reject whole parts of the menu out of hand without ever employing our speculative powers. We can get into the habit of always avoiding what is bad and we end up thinking about life this way; we order our minds to avoid some sort of perceived failure or negativity, just as we order our food from a place of anxiety: "What foods won't mess me up?" We can encounter thinking about existence the same way. Myself, or someone close to me, may have had a struggle with this or that in the past, so I live almost exclusively to avoid that or this. When in solitude, the mind gets ordered very often for avoidance. That is why we love diversion. So, the first move of contemplation is one of permissiveness. One must let the existential anguish, the misery of life, the problems, the fears, come to mind. Then they may be properly accounted for, and ordered. Think of Malcolm X's receptivity while in prison, how in his *Autobiography* he told of the experience of realizing his own moral emptiness, suggesting that all persons who grow intellectually and spiritually must acknowledge their pride, and enter humility. Or think of Eva Saulitis discovering the cancerous lump, the avoidance that had to transpire into acceptance, a rearrangement of her pattern, her story up to that point. We are limited, overwrought, pride-prone: just finite creatures. Coming to terms with that fact is necessary for a deeper understanding. A second step is then to take stock of the mind's own good. The mind is good, for from the very earliest cognitive processes, it facilitates recognitions of its own future (imagination), its experience (laws/patterns), and initiates change (freedom), all in the course of relational awareness. Contemplation is a permissive activity of the mind through which we allow some idea to re-order and re-prioritize what, or who, we think about. It is an encounter with the superlative, which then measures and transforms the patterns that captivate. We may need to re-examine the order of our mind's eye. This is an intentionality of thought. The intention is not to avoid the worst, but ordering our thought to consider what might be the best. The contemplative moment is an activity of the mind through which I allow whatever is good to structure and facilitate, to re-order the mind. By letting in the negative, the contemplative moment not only lets the truth of the human condition enter and be grasped but also another dimension, that which we may call the sacred or the spirit enters the struggle.

THE CALL TO CONTEMPLATION

This ordering process antedates Christianity, having been approached, considered, discussed, employed, and actualized from Socrates (d. 399 B.C.E.) to Plotinus (204/5–270 C.E.) and beyond. For his part, Aristotle concludes the *Nicomachean Ethics* with the argument that thinking as the gods think yields the best, and happiest, life. This is because, to his mind, the gods have no need of anything; they are content to understand all things. And those who have been called to contemplation, the philosophers, reflect the gods' penchant for thinking without distraction, since the gods are happily detached from legal tender, contracts, and the like. Also, Aristotle concludes that the intellect is the highest good in the human experience; and in the human intellect, the gods recognize themselves: they "delight in what is best and most akin to them."[2] This delight and enjoyment in thinking, contemplation, echoes some of what Aristotle considered about wonder; thinking delights because human potential is actualized in doing so. This ancient philosophical priority in contemplation can be interpreted as thinking that makes one aloof and privileged. To be so detached, attached to insights of leisure, offers an attractive alternative to both drudgery and

2. Aristotle, *Nicomachean Ethics*, 225–27.

politics. Contemplation can seem an escape in this case, and we see that digital detachment is forged on this ancient longing. This certainly is a risk in our encounters in contemplation. But if the object of our best thoughts is not only truth, but *love*, we are moved to active encounters of repair and restoration.

Twentieth-century philosopher Eric Voegelin (1901–85), in his *The Meditative Origin of the Philosophical Knowledge of Order*, has encapsulated this human struggle to think with transcendence as a movement. The human quest is a movement for intelligibility. And, the sacred is "a factor in the condition of being moved."[3] This is the encounter with reason's consistent movement and activation toward knowing, and the more passive and permissive intellection of being moved. Voegelin points out a tension in these movements due to the activity of the searching intellect and the passive condition of letting the sacred condition the search. This more passive condition of being moved is articulated in St. Paul's speech to the Athenians, naturally, in Acts 17:28: "For in Him we live and move and have our being." There, St. Paul suggests the abiding intimacy of the Divine, dwelling, as it were, and creating the condition for a movement into a new order of knowledge. The passive form of the Greek word he uses, *kinoumetha*, is a conjugation of the Greek *kineō*, to move, to set in motion. We derive kinesthetic from this word, and we have seen that both Thomas Merton's sitting cross-legged, Eva Saulitis' baptism performed by a cetacean, and Malcolm X's movements in prayer and Hajj involved this kinesthetic aspect; the body in contemplation is a particular type of movement. We are so moved. Walking, reading, listening: all can be happily conditioned by Another's movement. We must leave it to the theologians to grapple in order to determine at what ontological point, and to what degree, the human moves or is so moved by the Divine. Our concern here regards encounter, the movement *with*. For the word "contemplation" is a Latin compound, literally to *think with* the temple, with an open space. In each encounter of thought, this conjunctive and relational aspect of human reason has been amplified. In openness we relate and re-relate with patterns, with laws, and with our own capacity for novelty. In wonder, the encounter with nature and being envelops; in wonder we are aware that our individual being is reliant and contingent, along with all being. In that relationship we surmise in awe both the gift and limitations of the human prospect. In receptivity we come to the epitome of all other encounters

3. Voegelin, "The Meditative Origin," 47.

because, through the encounter with others, we learn the truth of our own experiences. If receptivity is the epitome of encounter, contemplation is the sum of every encounter in thought. If we acknowledge the possibility of the sacred dimension infusing our mental activity in order to apprehend the truth of things, then in that sort of recollection we have a summation of encounters; all others are concentrated under this activity of thinking with the Divine ground. This has at least three significant outcomes. We are properly ordered to intellectual humility, to intellectual self-trust and to a love of learning as we learn to love. The aimless struggle of our solitude, our intellectual pride, doubt, and ego are replanted in deeper, richer soil. Growing out of the enduring wounds of our reason is the bounty of humble insights, trusted speculations, and a curiosity filled with affection. Contemplation is a culmination of encounters in thought by which we go over the ground of experience with the Sacred in mind. We allow, as it were, God to get inside our heads.

CONTEMPLATION EXEMPLIFICATION: ST. ANSELM

In what follows, we enter into a different context for reason. This context is one in which openness, wonder, and receptivity are interpreted in terms that are more elemental and pared down to their most simple state. This may become a struggle for us, since the encounter with our own minds is whittled down to its most basic, without the premonitions and prospects of relevance and practicality, instrumental and utilitarian reason. This consideration of eleventh-century brilliance may leave us feeling as though life is nothing more than flirting with the edges of vagueness and irrelevance. By the chapter's end, we will have struggled with parsing the grammar of ideation and reality. There is no better guide than St. Anselm. Anselm provides signs of how contemplation reads us because he shows us how to engage the sense we have of the enigmatic.

In 1047, St. Anselm had his first stirrings of the call to become a monk. Thirteen years later he entered the monastery at Bec in what is now northern France. He left his home in Aosta, Italy, in 1056 after feuds with his father; his mother had died in 1050. He left northern Italy and went through the Rhone Valley into southern France. He traveled for three years and found himself at the Benedictine monastery in Bec in 1059, where he would study under Lafranc, a strong leader and administrator. Though having very different temperaments, Anselm would follow Lafranc as prior of

Bec (1063) and, after serving as abbot there, eventually as Archbishop of Canterbury (1093). After exile from England, a mandate of King Henry I, he returned to his duties as Archbishop in 1106, three years later he would fall ill and die at the age of seventy-six.

According to one of his biographers, Anselm lived through one of "the most momentous periods of change in European history."[4] This period's transitions involved at least three significant aspects.

First, science was encroaching on the singular focus of theological tradition, asserting itself in controversy, notably that between Anselm's teacher Lafranc and Berenger of Tours, who would interrogate the church's teaching on the Eucharist, suggesting there was room for more symbolic interpretation of the bread and the wine.[5] Since these were epistemological questions, questions about how we come to know matters and the truth of matters, there was a renewed sense of the power of reason to interrogate religious doctrine.

Secondly, the ideological stability of Europe, under the theological structure of the church, was facing challenges from Islam, which now occupied the Holy Land. Then too, there was a renewal of Jewish thought and culture.

Third, the pattern and spirit of education was in flux. Anselm is an emblem of the period of monastic learning, when contemplation, teaching, and learning formed a unity of purpose. The Cathedral School at Paris was quite young. That school inaugurated a new epoch of educational aims and methods. Though monastic theology and scholastic theology shared obvious objects of inquiry (e.g., Scripture); monastic learning was unequivocally a search for God and all liturgical and social activities served this primary goal. A newly established university like the one at Paris, had an altogether different atmosphere, symbolized by geometric symmetry, gothic architecture, expressed in mathematical terms. Dialectic reason overtook a more liturgical context for learning. While the monastic learning was focused on the quest for God, the debates of the scholastics developed a precision through which dialectical reason, not solely reasoning with God through prayer, would become more and more influential.

Highly conscious of these new challenges and patterns, yet resolute in his commitment to the heart of the church's monastic mission, Anselm

---

4. Southern, *St. Anselm*, xxvii–xxix, 4.

5. For an overview of the metaphysical problem, see Southern, *St. Anselm*, 46–50.

presents to our historical context a highly sensitive thinker who can teach us about the need for, and aim of, contemplation.

For his part, Anselm "aimed at giving new clarity to ancient truths."[6] Below, we explore just three of these truths which address the contemporary context. These are: the mind as created for a participation in divine reason; the order of the contemplative mind in the sphere of politics; and, a renewed appreciation of the human being and the stewardship of all being led by Anselm's method, namely, the invitation to *believe in order to understand*. According to Emery Gyulai, Anselm's faith enjoyed a "qualified priority" in his thinking in that "it is the wellspring of wisdom and the corrective for all cognitional undertakings."[7] This is a premise that orients all thought, since trust in the intelligibility of reality, nature, and truth can guide us in an age of fragmentation.

PONDEROUSNESS IN THE MONOLOGUE

Actors often audition for parts by performing a monologue, speaking a large amount of a script written for a character that reveals that character's virtues, vices, obsessions, and humor. A monologue in this sense is thinking "out loud" in order to work out whatever is impinging upon oneself or others as a problem, issue, concern. In short, what things mean in that particular narrative. A monologue is a particular kind of learning event. There is a sense of speaking in order to get to the bottom of something, to its source. The mind becomes ordered to ascertain underlying causes. The character may be responding to a particular question, or reflecting in a different context about what some other character had said, or done. Anselm's most famous philosophical works, *The Monologion* and *The Proslogion*, were written in response to requests. These requests were made by fellow monks who, aware of the changing perception of the role of reason, faith, and knowledge, wanted a treatise on the coherence of Christianity without recourse to Scripture or the authorities from the past. *The Monologion* is Anselm's first response. It is so titled because in the work, Anselm sets out to write a "soliloquy," utilizing his own reason and without any explicit intercessions, petitions, or doxologies to the God who is the subject of the

6. Southern, *St. Anselm*, 53. On the transition from monastic to scholastic emphasis, their similarities and differences, see Gaál Gyulai, *The Art of Equanimity*, 95–101. And for the European context for Anselm, see Gaál Gyulai, *The Art of Equanimity*, 353–55.

7. Gaál Gyulai, *The Art of Equanimity*, 362.

treatise. Even if we sense that the subject, as it were, overhears the mono-logue, Anselm does not enter the dialogical theology that characterizes his *Proslogion*, fashioned after St. Augustine's *Confessions*. So, in the *Monolo-gion* we have an extended meditation on the nature of reason in relation to God, and this reflection invites us into a contemplative moment in order to become ever more cognizant of the nature and order of our human minds. Consider the eleventh century in relation to the twenty-first. In both, the nature of reason is contentious. And in both centuries a new science of rea-son pervades claims to knowledge, understanding, and truth. A reflection on reason's role and purpose in all human endeavors was necessary then, as now. Think too of the twenty-first century "nones," the spiritual-but-not-religious demographic that sit in classrooms, those for whom the words "religion" or "church" evoke an alien image, or simply alienation. By re-sponding to his fellow monks' requests for a treatise explaining something of the sacred without recourse to authority or Scripture, Anselm provides a blueprint from which people of faith might construct new knowledge of an old fact, that some of our best thinking is infused with the numinous.[8]

Modernity's thinking, and to certain extent thinking with devices, is thinking as a self-enclosed cell among other impenetrable cells. This think-ing can lead to loneliness or consumerist-fed identity, what Albert Borg-mann calls "ambiguous individualism." In the *Monologion*, Anselm begins a discussion of reason's relation to God by focusing the mind exocentrically, to the things that surround and encompass us, focusing on the good of creation.[9] Anselm invites people to consider their own capacity to judge the world around them, to consider what their senses desire, and see that there is a diversity of things that are good, whose qualities are recognized as valu-able. A horse, for example, is good, not only because it is beautiful, but also because it is swift and strong.[10] Furthermore, Anselm invites any person to consider how one judges between different goods. What is good may

8. The numinous, explored in relation to religious experience by Rudolf Otto, signi-fies the unique state of mind of a religious person who feels awe and wonder, a sense of awareness of the Divine presence.

9. Borgmann, *Crossing the Postmodern Divide*, 37–47. Borgmann's analysis of post-modern selfhood involves a consumerist-driven individualism; it is ambiguous because one can decide, through consumerist choices, who to become. The other two aspects of postmodern identity, for Borgmann are: methodical universalism—efficiency thinking for the bottom line, and aggressive realism, alleviating human misery through techno-logical innovation, but negatively, the manipulation and destruction of nature for human ends.

10. Anselm, *Proslogion*, 37–39.

be compared with what is better, or best. A swift and strong robber is not good, yet the qualities of swift and strong applied to a horse are good because a swift and strong horse is useful. Seeing that which is useful, Anselm suggests that when we consider the things that encompass us, we are led to the question of their source. Our minds are ordered to get to the bottom of these matters. Where do these things come from, what makes them, what makes them good? When something is contingent on something else, like horses, rocks, streams, etc., it cannot exist through itself, and therefore it is less than that which created it. In inviting reason to consider the Source of all that is, Anselm is also claiming that creation is good by degrees, and the highest degree of good can only exist in the Source of all that exists.

> It follows, therefore, that all other goods are good through another being than that which they themselves are, and this being alone is good through itself. Hence, this alone is supremely good, which is alone good through itself. For it is supreme, in that it so surpasses other beings, that it is neither equaled nor excelled. But that which is supremely good is also supremely great. There is therefore, some one being which is supremely good, and supremely great, that is, the highest of all existing beings.[11]

The move from interior, to exterior, to the Source of all, is a result of encounter: encounter with nature and human nature, the perceiver of nature; encounter with things and their ultimate Source. All inquiry, as we see, is relational in the sense that being encompasses us in its manifold goodness. Intelligence moves beyond itself in order to ascertain the environment and to judge what is good therein. A sort of natural inclination, Anselm points out, is to wonder about the Source of everything. We are left to consider, however, the source of the mind itself. Since we come to inquire about the source of things, we will come to inquire about the source of the mind itself, the source of the reason that so judges what is good by degrees and speculates as to the Source of all that is. Both the deer and the human being can discern brackish from clear water. The human, however, is able to make brackish water clear, or engineer nature so as to insure water's health. Not only is the quality of water understood, its purpose and meaning are discerned as well. But more, its significance for life is preserved. If such care is a resource of the human mind, what is its source? Another way to put it: what is it about human reason that understands the health of creation?

11. Anselm, *Proslogion*, 40.

Since Anselm wants to provide a coherent way to articulate the reality of God in a time of transition, he argues that every thinking person is able to consider the Source of existence, and, in being elevated to the question of the One Source of all reason, that very consideration constitutes a common participation in the One, the Divine. When we conceive God as the Source of all there is, we imitate the One who conceived creation. Human reason, in so conceiving, is led and re-sourced by the One God, the highest good.

> Therefore, the mind may most fitly be said to be its own mirror wherein it contemplates, so to speak, the image of what it cannot see face to face. For, if the mind itself, alone among all created beings is capable of remembering and conceiving of, and loving itself, I do not see why it should be denied that it is the true image of that being which, through its memory and intelligence and love, is united in an ineffable Trinity.[12]

To contemplate is to order the mind to reflect the mind of God in conception, in remembering, and loving. But Anselm biographer R. W. Southern has said of the *Monologion*: "it was intended as a guide to those willing to submit to its discipline."[13] This is because Anselm consistently argues that it is a voluntary act of thinking that strengthens this image. "It is clear, then, that the rational creature ought to devote its whole ability and will to remembering, and conceiving of, and loving, the supreme good for which end it recognizes that it has its very existence."[14] There is a moral choice involved here, a willingness to offer time to this thinking of, and with, Another. Our encounter in this order of thought demands a careful and attentive disposition. For in the very process of reflection on the greatest Good, the human patterns of thought that distract and detract from this movement toward the Good are exposed for what they are.

> What is more obvious, then, than that the more earnestly the rational mind devotes itself to learning its own nature, the more effectively does it rise to the knowledge of that Being; and the more carelessly it contemplates itself, the farther does it descend from the contemplation of the that Being.[15]

---

12. Anselm, *Proslogion*, 132.

13. Southern, *St. Anselm*, 124.

14. Anselm, *Proslogion*, 133–34.

15. Anselm, *Proslogion*, 132.

Ordering our mind toward God is a stark encounter with our feeble-ness and fragility. We relate to ourselves in a novel way due to the relation with the superlative Nature from which we are derived. Our experience of thinking recapitulates our thinking about experience in this Anselmian rendering, giving it a new form. In gaining new access to the structure of our minds, we have partial access to God's. We renew the order of our minds in relation to our Source.

The monastic context of the *Monologion* gives us a sense of Anselm's personality, namely, that he shares his wisdom, born of his own struggles with experiencing God through his commitment. In other words, he speaks from his own experience of struggle and offers guidance to his brethren who have requested a way to think through the reality of their lives. The eleventh-century monastic context of struggling, avoiding carelessness in disciplined thought and action, is especially instructive for us, since our capacity for careful thought and thinking of supreme matters is consistently compromised by distraction. Yet the scope of human reason, its fundamen-tal disposition as relational, crosses the centuries, and in Anselm we can recognize clearly the innate desire to order reason to what is best, and to the Source of every good thing. The reader, the pilgrim, the listener is disposed more competently to their tasks, when they attend to learning their own nature, and in so doing, learn also something of the Source of their nature.

CONTEMPLATIVE ORDER AND THE POLITICAL PATTERN

It is likely, however, that in so ordering the mind in this way habitually, we confront the patterns that condition much of the surrounding culture. The encounter with patterns, then, will evoke emotional and intellectual tension. The *Monologion* was written fifteen years after Anselm took vows as a monk and two years later, in 1078, he was elected abbot of the mon-astery. Eighteen years later he would become Archbishop of Canterbury. His thirty-three years as a monk, guiding others in the contemplative life while giving to the history of philosophy an enduring and profound expres-sion of reasonable faith, served mostly to galvanize his recognition that the world of politics and governance was not the most ideal place for a man of his temperament. In this way we see that when the order won in con-templation encounters the intransigent patterns of politics, economics, and conquest, that order measures and sifts those patterns, mostly by resisting them. According to Southern, St. Anselm's leadership as the Archbishop of Canterbury had no "unity of policy" because he had no policy or agenda to actualize. Rather, his leadership was a "unity of holiness."[16] There are three examples from St. Anselm's contemplative leadership that give us a sense of how the order of contemplation encounters the patterns of political action.

First, the earliest biographer of Anselm, Eadmer, was also his mentee, confidant, and fellow monk. The first version of Eadmer's biography was finished just three to five years after Anselm's death. Since it was written by such a close friend, we have a credible witness to Anselm's mind, behavior, and temperament. Eadmer reports that Anselm was distraught often by the political wrangling with kings, bishops, those in his inner circle, and his administrative tasks, particularly the preservation of properties. Some of those monks who were close to Anselm when he became Archbishop, took advantage of his kindliness and trust. An extended quote from Eadmer gives us the sense of the contemplative's disposition in the midst of such wrangling:

> Secular business however was something which he could not patiently abide, and he used every pretext to withdraw himself from it as far as he could. But if some case came up at which it was necessary for him to be present, his only concern was for the truth, and he would not allow anyone to be deceived or injured in anything connected to his affairs. When useless uproars, controversies, and altercations arose, as sometimes happens, he tried either to stem them or to get out as quickly as possible. For unless he did this, he was immediately overcome with weariness; his spirits drooped, and he even ran the risk of serious illness. When long experience had taught us this tendency of his, we drew him out of the crowd when such occasion arose and put to him some question of Holy Scripture; and so we brought his body and mind back to their accustomed state, restored to health by this sort of wholesome anti-dote.[17]

Such witness may tell us as much about Eadmer as it does about Anselm. Eadmer's preventative medicine—to put a question to Anselm in order to bring his mind and body "to their accustomed state"—gives us a snapshot of how recollecting the ultimate matters of God and humanity can edify and uplift in the midst of stress. Two other things are worth our notice. Anselm's thirty years as a contemplative did *not* make him patient

16. Southern, *St. Anselm*, xxvii, 232.

17. Eadmer, *The Life of St. Anselm*, viii, 80–81.

with everything. But when duty called, his primary concerns were for truth and care of those for whom he was responsible. Having been appointed to his administrative post, Anselm reluctantly engaged in the difficult tasks of negotiating power. Eadmer helps us to see that, for a contemplative like Anselm, the power of truth and care took the better part of Anselm's administrative mind. A leader who intentionally cares for the moral order of his mind can be frustrating for those being led and those the leader is obligated to negotiate with. But also, the contemplative leader becomes frustrated with him or herself. Could it be that the leader becomes impacted by the patterns she must engage? This could be the case, especially due to the moral priorities ordered and discerned, which often clash with the established patterns of culture. This sort of tension may be inevitable in the synergy between contemplation and action, order and pattern.

Secondly, Anselm was respectful of royal leadership, but never did give full "homage" to Kings William Rufus or Henry I. In 1094, Rufus would call on Anselm to provide monetary support for his attack on Normandy. Though on good terms with the king, Anselm was cautious about providing support. Nonetheless, Anselm made an offer of five hundred pounds. The king demanded more, and asked Anselm for one thousand pounds. At that point Anselm refused to offer any support, turned around, and gave the five hundred pounds to the poor.[18]

Third, when Henry I became king, Anselm refused to even ceremonially give him homage. And after Henry's coronation, Anselm refused to consecrate the bishops whom Henry had invested with bishoprics. According to Southern, this was not so much a personal refusal on the part of Anselm as it was Anselm's obedience to the pope and recent papal decrees. In Anselm's mind, then, obedience to church was higher on the order of matters than obedience to regional powers; he was doing his duty based on his thoroughly worked-out order of obedience. King Henry, of course, exiled him as a result, and Anselm found himself on the run.[19]

CONTEMPLATING MAXIMAL GREATNESS

When in encounter with one's own mind and the Divine, the mind is ordered to value; this is the area of moral philosophy. Encounters in thought yield insights into discerning the good. In the history of the West, royalty

18. Southern, *St. Anselm*, 272.

19. Southern, *St. Anselm*, 292.

has been more or less great. The chair of Peter, also, has been occupied by popes who were more or less great. Anselm thought it *better* to obey the pope, and best to obey God. We assume that is why he went into the monastery in the first place. Thomas Merton thought it would be better to maintain his vow of celibacy than to marry. Eva Saulitis knew it would be better for her to study biology than music, even though her talent was well-suited to the music conservancy. Malcolm X seemed to respect his teacher Mr. Ostrowski, but knew better than to heed his racist advice. He perceived Elijah Mohammed as honorable, but developed a deeper respect for the greatness of universal Islam, and of course, Allah, the Greatest of all. De-vices are great for communication, but the software engineers who develop them are greater. Ants are great workers, but dogs have greater intelligence. Nations can be more or less great, but they must have great citizens and know the true source of greatness. How many bar conversations are there about the greatest catcher in the history of Major League Baseball? The best U.S. president or the greatest all around NBA player? (Magic Johnson, of course.) All of being is measured by degrees of bad, good, better, and best. Great, greater, greatest. That which is greatest draws us on to what is better, ad infinitum. Twenty-five years before King Henry I seized the Archbishop's lands and exiled him, Anselm had written the *Proslogion,* a prayerful dis-course containing the highly influential so-called "ontological argument," a really beautiful, meditative, logical, and quite captivating consideration of being to the highest degree, also known as maximal greatness. Linda Zagzebski points out that, among modern philosophers, the ontological argument "continues to fascinate." She also distinguishes Anselm's proof as the only classical argument that is "purely a priori." Which means that it contains no premise "acquired from experience."[20] She further explicates what both Reformed author Karl Barth, and, after him, Thomas Merton suggested: that twentieth-century interpretations of the "argument" failed to see the writing in its proper context, one of prayer and meditation. Za-gzebski puts it this way: "It is unlikely that Anselm intended the argument to answer either agnostic inquirers or atheistic attackers."[21] Modern phi-losophy, shorn of its duty to become conscious, aware, and understanding of the complex factors that provide context for all thought, has tended to

20. Zagzebski, *Philosophy of Religion,* 48.

21. Zagzebski, *Philosophy of Religion,* 49. For Thomas Merton's refreshing teaching on the significance of Anselm for both contemplative life, tradition, and philosophical theology, see Merton, *Cistercian Fathers and Fore-fathers,* 41–134.

reduce the ontological argument to a perplexing, and for some, fun, exercise in logical reasoning. It certainly is that, but with the guiding words of its author, we can discern an offering, born of days of intellectual struggle, and an invitation, born of a loving heart that wants all people to experience the wonder inherent in our speculative powers, and the reality of the God of love. Listen to the first words of the first chapter. (What the history of Western philosophy has called the ontological argument is in the second chapter.)

> Up now, slight man! Flee, for a little while, thy occupations; hide thyself, for a time, from thy disturbing thoughts. Cast aside, now, thy burdensome cares, and put away thy toilsome business. Yield room for some little time for God; and rest for a little time for him. Enter the inner chamber of thy mind; shut out all thoughts save that of God, and such as can aid thee in seeking him; close thy door and seek him. Speak now, my whole heart! Speak now to God, saying, I seek thy face . . . .[22]

These words of Anselm are preparatory words, words of anticipation. Displace those disturbing patterns of thought and emplace *that than which nothing greater can be conceived*. Not only is thought conditioned by the way we live, but here, it is conditioned by mystical awareness, the numinous. Philosophy and religion are never so easily distinguished. The modern temperament does not like costume parties, but perhaps the postmodern temperament does? Prepare for an encounter with God, mediated by imagination and logic: an encounter that invites reason to openness, wonder, and receptivity. Rather than lay out a syllogism or offer line-by-line commentary, I would like to put Anselm's ideas forth by connecting them to openness, wonder, and receptivity. If we connect the "proof" to our themes, then we assume that thought is an encounter, a relational prospect for learning. It is here, then, that we believe in order to understand, as Anselm presumed. Thus, we take Anselm's writing as he intended, an undergoing, as it were. That means that it is not so much a defense or a proof in modernity's sense. It is an invitation to contemplate, to think through the implications of the mind's capacity for both speculation and precision.

Can we be open, first, to Anselm's invitation to the state of vulnerability and belief in the quote above? If so, we can begin to enter the logic of a mindful way to approach God. As the second chapter of the *Proslogion* demonstrates, we also need to be open to Anselm's proposal, namely,

22. Anselm, *Proslogion*, 3.

that he would want us to agree that we can define God as that than which nothing greater can be conceived. Is there an opening here? God is that than which nothing greater can be conceived. Perhaps that is too much too fast. Or, we are skeptical that there is such a nature. So, the conversation is closed off at the first premise if we do not at least entertain the proposal. But Anselm would want to open us to another idea. Even if you think there is no such nature, a being than which nothing greater can be conceived, you can still understand the meaning of that definition of God. So, that proposal or definition of God as "that than which nothing greater can be conceived" can at least be understood by all people. Can you imagine the greatest possible being? That is what his proposal is inviting us to do. So, let us be open to the possibility that there could be a being that is greatest of all other beings. So, it may be that someone doesn't think that God exists but they can agree that the definition or idea of God is in their understanding. If we are open to this, then what we know at this point is that Anselm wants us to consider God as that than which nothing greater can be conceived, and, if the non-believer cannot agree that this being exists, at the least he can agree that the definition is understood and is in his understanding. Opening further that distinction, Anselm provides an example.

> When a painter first conceives of what he will afterwards perform, he has it in his understanding, but he does not yet understand it to be, because he has not performed it. But after he has made the painting, he both has it in his understanding and he understands that it exists, because he has made it.[23]

So, it is clear, then, that what exists in the understanding does not necessarily exist in reality. But now, we need to enter into a bit of wonder about Anselm's definition. God is that than which nothing greater can be conceived. It is clear from chapter 1 of the *Proslogion*, that the God Anselm is talking about is the greatest in mercy, love, justice, truth, compassion, the Creator, Redeemer, Sustainer. Anselm knew his first readers would know that when he speaks about the greatest being, this would be their frame of reference. The compassion of Dorothy Day or Desmond Tutu is great, but the source of their compassion must be greater. The creativity of human invention is great, but divine creativity is much, much greater. We move by degrees to the very limit of our capacity to grasp the scale and scope of Being. But we can also say, in wonder, that Dorothy Day and Desmond Tutu

23. Anselm, *Proslogion*, 7.

never thought or acted alone; they had encounters in thought and action. Emery Gyulai suggests that if Anselm were able to counter rational atheism he would do it "[w]ith the observation that all thinking moves within the parameters of an inherent dynamics, which endows that endeavor with purpose. There is contained in every thought a thrust conveying the certain feeling to the thinker that he/she is not alone in his/her house, let alone its master."[24] The idea that God is "that than which nothing greater can be conceived" gets our speculative powers moving, and accompanies our inquisitive tendencies toward the limit of human reason. Again, Gyulai, inspired by Anselm's eleventh-century work, fuses reason and mysticism in this statement: "It may well be that the inquisitive mind arrives at a rather strange insight but no impasse: it is able to admit the utter incomprehensibility of the sought object and yet to *recognize* it precisely as incomprehensible and ineffable."[25] Thinking of maximal greatness makes us wonder, and in that wondering we acknowledge our human *incapacity* to know God in God's fullness. Nonetheless, we do have the capacity to recognize ineffability. We might call it an intimate enigma of the mind. It evokes wonder.

So, we are open to Anselm's definition, open to the distinction between something existing in the understanding and something existing in reality. And we can entertain, and perhaps are entertained by, the wonder of our speculative inquiries into conceiving of the greatest possible Being. Now, to be receptive to this point we have to receive this fact: that than which nothing greater can be conceived exists in the understanding, *at least*. We can say at this point that God is at least, or merely, an idea. But the implications of God existing at least in the understanding must also be *received*.

For when we truly receive the definition for this idea that Anselm gives to us, that God is that than which nothing greater can be conceived, we are unable to say "that than which nothing greater can be conceived is merely an idea." An idea is *less than* "that than which nothing greater can be conceived." It would amount to saying that than which nothing greater can be conceived is not actually that than which nothing greater can be conceived. This is a contradiction. If something is that which nothing greater can be conceived it must be greater than an idea, in fact, for maximal greatness entails existence. "It cannot be conceived not to exist."[26] That than which nothing greater can be conceived *necessarily exists in reality*. Here, the mind

24. Gaál Gyulai, *The Art of Equanimity*, 360.

25. Gaál Gyulai, *The Art of Equanimity*, 356 (emphasis in original).

26. Anselm, *Proslogion*, 8.

is held accountable to its own operations, namely, that something cannot be what it is, and what it is not, at the same time. Further, the mind is ordered to attend to the implications of ideas; that if we agree to certain ideas, those ideas entail practical inevitabilities. If one agrees with Anselm's definition, there are certain implications of that definition that demand that we concur with his conclusion. Thinking about value, the greatest Being, impacts the meaning of the mind, nature and culture.

BELIEVE IN ORDER TO UNDERSTAND

When we believe in order to understand we enter into a relational encounter and evolve a new order of the mind which interprets afresh old patterns. When an infant displaces itself, developing its imaginative capacities in anticipation of parental concern, we see the fruit of relational encounter *de novo*. The infant believes in order to understand. By and large, modern science is premised on a different methodology, whereby understanding must be won first, then we have reason to believe. This is rooted in experiential or experimental processes by which we come to appreciate the patterns that are evident and then explain how those patterns work. The relational aspect to the object of study is downplayed to a very great degree, since abstraction can produce a more objective picture of how things work. Evolutionary biology is an example of this process of understanding in order to believe. This method is also bent toward such care and precision, bordering on certainty, that the scientist could remain enclosed somewhat in the vestiges of abstraction. Not only does the present era not appreciate the great care the scientist takes to come to some reasonable belief, but there is a correlative apathy to the expert's discovered truth. And yet, the scientist cut from this method will rarely assert with the boldness of businessmen or politicians, the unequivocal conclusion of this method; it is just not, as it were, in their DNA. In this method of scientific discovery, value always takes a back seat to the foregoing discovery. But the history of technology tells a different story.

Prospecting for oil, gold, natural gas; these involve science, but in the prospector's mind, there is a pre-scientific and imaginative, say speculative, operation at work. The prospector believes in order to understand. And that belief is the mother of invention, of coils, wires, wells, and conduits. What we call computer science is of this prospecting nature. Someone believed that everyone should be able to hold a super-computer in the palm of their hands. Someone believed that the grid-work of military computing could be bought and sold as email, then internet. Computer science and engineering are driven by market forces; thereby they have the same form: believe in order to understand. In the business world this amounts to: "just do it and ask for forgiveness later." So, someone believes that artificial intelligence is the next innovative and transformative key to civilization. The implications will be worked out later, even the moral implications, because someone believes that AI is an inevitability. Someone believes that nations can be great again. But there seems to be little time spent understanding either the past of those nations, or, the current realities, which are very different from nostalgia, which can often blur our retrospective imaginations.

Genuine receptivity and contemplation mean that we integrate both of these methodologies into our everyday living. We thereby develop a holistic picture of the way things are. When we experience our thinking, and think about our experience, we capitalize on both believing in order to understand and understanding in order to believe. Thus, we come to some intellectual self-trust, knowing that there are valid truths to be discovered in reasonably worked-out beliefs, and beliefs that lead to deeper understanding. I want to suggest that belief in God, and particularly, the maximal greatness of God, can measure the utopian visions of artificial intelligence, and the self-enclosed certainty of those who conclude that understanding in order to believe is the only game in town. St. Anselm's believing in order to understand God's greatness leads to a proper intellectual humility. In this case, maximal greatness orders our values.

Believing in the greatest possible Being has implications for understanding all other matters, notably time, human limitations, and the role of historically contingent people for the future health of the planet. Believing *in* something is different from believing *that* something. I believe *in* God, a relational sort of knowing. I believe *that* evolutionary biology offers the most probable explanation for the development of life on earth. Certainly, my relationship to evolutionary biology is different from my relationship with God. Believing *in* that than which nothing greater can be conceived involves an investment of my whole being, my reason, heart, imagination, and speculative powers. Believing *that* evolutionary biology offers the most probable explanation for the development of life on earth takes an investment on my part, but not the same kind of integrative investment. Even an evolutionary biologist who is a dog owner believes *in* his dog's unconditional regard for him, the dog's loving obedience, and his dog's inability to hold a grudge. He feels responsible for the dog and the dog's future. He also believes *that* dogs evolved from wolves. Those are two different experiences of understanding.[27]

But the encounter with maximal greatness has another side-effect for understanding. It places time itself in perspective, my time in particular as radically limited, and, future times as dependent upon present conditions. St. Anselm lived for seventy-six years, one thousand years after Christ, and about one thousand years before you took up this book into your hands, or onto your reading device. Presently, he stands at the center of the (so-called) Christian centuries up to this point in time, between the ancient world and the digital one; not quite medieval, and about five hundred years after the beginnings of Islam. The care Anselm took in offering an account of Christian belief without authorities/tradition is not unlike the ancient Christians who had to open out the boundaries of cultures and traditions to synergize an awareness of new possibilities in the social order. Today, though our era is distinct in technological innovation, we still read Anselm because of his adeptness in conserving the very best of reason's intentionality, to encounter being, and Being. In so doing all other powers are measured against the truth of the One in philosophical terms, the absolute. In the reasonable encounter with that Eternal One, two hundred years of modern technological innovation seem underwhelming, especially in light of the horrors of slavery, the holocaust, and ecological degradation.

Throughout these past two thousand years, people like Anselm and Merton, Saulitis and Malcolm X have interrupted patterns in order to conserve and preserve something of value. I borrow these definitions from the U.S. National Park service: conservation is the proper use of nature; preservation is the protection of nature from use.[28] For Anselm, the monastic life was to be undertaken because it conserves the prospect of human nature as humble, charitable, pure, and simple. And, for him, the monastic life was to be undertaken because it preserves in historical contingencies the freedom necessary to insure the truth of human existence: that we are made for love. Eternity tends to place our historical context in its proper perspective. In our frenetic age, what are we seeking to preserve and conserve? How does this civilization measure against Anselm's? Or that which produced Islam five hundred years prior to Anselm? The innovations of the device

---

27. For the distinction see Marcel, *The Mystery of Being, Vol II: Faith and Reality*, 77.

28. *National Park Service.* https://www.nps.gov/klgo/learn/education/classrooms/conservation-vs-preservation.htm

paradigm seem a bit over-rated to me, especially as we consider they have tended to mitigate relational awareness and genuine human encounters of concern. Contemplation that interrupts the cultural patterns by recapitulating experience, ordering it to maximal greatness has the potential to renew human endeavors, endeavors rooted in love: of nature, of culture of God.

CONTEMPLATION APPLIED: ENTERING SILENCE

"Silence is not the absence of something but the presence of everything."

—GORDON HEMPTON

The great twentieth century philosopher Ludwig Wittgenstein finished his *Tractatus Logico Philosophicus* with these words: "What we cannot speak about we must pass over in silence."[29] His concern, of course, was that people, and philosophers especially, should not speak on matters they do not know about. Wittgenstein helps us to appreciate that thinking logically is primarily a *moral* activity. His statement demonstrates an important truth: when a person restrains their speech they reveal, at least to themselves, their deep moral commitment. For such restraint is a moral action of a very high caliber because the action is carried out "in secret."[30] Passing over in silence certainly does not mean we stop thinking, or stop seeking knowledge; it simply means we have integrity and humility, that's all. Our own awareness of what we do not know can reduce us to silence. How much more, with Anselm, should our partial knowledge of God so reduce us? With God, however, it seems an invitation, not a restraint. Whether self-restraint or response to invitation, perhaps both, the result of entering intentionally into silence evolves a deeper way of knowing.

THE DIN OF INSTRUMENTAL REASON

The digital culture's remove from silence might astound St. Anselm. This context is obviously riven with the noises only a global economic system

---

29. Wittgenstein, *Tractatus*, 89. For an interpretation of Wittgenstein's religious point of view, See Fergus Kerr, *Theology After Wittgenstein*, 36–45.

30. Matt 6:4–6.

can make. But also, instead of having a rule that says that entering silence is mandatory and necessary for the essential identity of a monk, contemporary society understands silence as a sign of a weak mind: someone who is silent is someone who has no sense of the necessity and importance of all manner of information, data, or whatever is thought to be relevant. For St. Anselm, silence meant goodness, obedience, authenticity. For digital culture, silence means dispossession, insignificance, irrelevance. Smart people should always have something to say. Yet the more noise that belches forth from industrialization, and now, digital media, the more it becomes apparent that we're all rather confused. When we stop talking, consuming and communicating, we can arrive at the ocean of our ignorance. We can even stick our toes into the water, and we are thus introduced to a nano-percentage of what we have been missing.

Acoustic ecology is the study of the natural sounds of places, places so rare these days that Gordon Hempton has spent the last thirty years working to preserve these places, soundscapes free of human noise.[31] This kind of preservation and protection is a highly specialized form of environmental ethics, since the consumptive economy tends to make a lot of noise. Cultivating quiet places necessarily limits consumption. The quieter the place, the less ecological destruction. So the logic goes. In the quote from Hempton above we have a student of natural silence corroborating the contemplative's disposition. For in the contemplative's silence, as we have seen, all the thoughts, the presence of everything, appears and is evaluated. The finite, the not-so-good, the evil, it is permitted within; thereby we search for the stillness that transcends and amends everything else.

If we have become pliant, made malleable by constant activity and digital consumption, the threshold of silence is not a door; it is more like a wall with barbed wire. The consistently distracted person will be repelled, not allured, by the threshold of silence. For many, silence is awkward. In this case silence must be introduced by another. If my seven-year-old son is asking about whether birds recycle, I can add, "See if you can listen to the birds singing." Just as children in food deserts don't know what a cucumber is, children whose lives are filled with noise have no idea what a woodpecker sounds like.

Parents and teachers today have to interrupt digital patterns out of the necessity of conservation. The conservation of the environment is bound up with the conservation of natural and human silence. Wonder is elicited

31. Goodman, "Quiet Please: Gordon Hempton on the Search for Silence," 6.

by natural things, and the elemental: sky, earth, rain, lightning. The curious want to be quiet in order to appreciate, and understand. Silence is the human elemental, the first principle of learning. We measure our thoughts and restrain our desire to be heard. It is difficult to find the time for such experiences, contemplative experiences. Though we can develop a competence in becoming still even as we read, walk, and listen, it takes a willful intentionality to do so. That kind of intentionality can be sketched in common terms, inside and outside.

SUPERINTENDING WITHIN, WITHOUT

Intentional reading, walking, and listening are voluntary actions in that we *will* the activity and become freely responsible for stewarding the action. Stewarding silence is no different, for silence is something we must enter into. It is difficult today to approach the threshold of silence, let alone enter into it. Yet consciousness seems emplaced, positioned between that which encompasses us and interiority. Anselm has invited us to consider that the nature of that interiority is derived from the One Source that also crafted the nature that encompasses us, therefore, thinking is always conjunctive, that is, *with*. If we have this dimension as a rational nature, it is consistently exo-centric in order to thrive and survive. Silence is a way to pursue this nature, as a part of nature itself, in order to allow, as Gilson has said, being to encompass us. The threshold of silence is consistently in view. In busyness we get used to seeing it as a revolving door, however, rather than as a portal to a fertile, verdant field.

We live perceiving what is without; we think things through, bringing reason to bear inwardly, within. We use the language of an idea being "in the back of my mind." Ideas are within. Or, conversely, the effort to be objective and observational, the perceptual stimulants come from without. Perception takes on this spatial aspect as apprehension is from without, from within. When focused solely on externals, say on appearances, we live on the "surface." When we enter more intentionally introspective processes, we go in, beneath the surface. Digital patterns generally keep us distracted with surfaces. We may say that our digital culture courts a skimming and surfacey kind of life; a living without living within. If we examine the phrase, *living without living within*, the word *without* serves as a negation, not necessarily a reference to externals. Living without living within amounts to not being attendant to the introspective pull. But when we add a comma to the phrase, we have a more accurate depiction of a balanced consciousness, of order and pattern, of contemplation and action, of externals and internals *in simultaneity*. The rationality we objectify as inwardness or sense perception is rather expansive, neither all in nor all out. By intending such contemplative balance, we are *living without, living within*. We engage that which encompasses us from without while simultaneously reflecting inwardly on this engagement. The pause inscribed by the comma makes all the difference. That comma is the threshold of silence; when we *enter* silence the comma becomes an ellipsis. An ellipsis in this sense of punctuation, signifies the omission of words in a sentence to get . . . to the substance of what the sentence is attempting to express. Silence works analogously, doesn't it? We omit words, wordiness, in order to enter deeply the substance of our experience.

When we do enter that silence, however, the clutter of our minds ensues; thinking becomes less *metanoia* and more paranoia.[32] But a deeper stillness listens to the din of that chatter from an adjacent vantage point; we can listen in on it and *let it go*, for God is *with* us. What we are letting pass on are the patterns of our thought that have been instantiated through the routine of experience. The adjacent vantage point in stillness is the beginning of order, re-ordering so that the patterns fade, no longer interminable. A Zen koan is helpful here: "only when there is stillness in movement can the universal rhythm appear."[33]

TIME WILLING

Stillness can be found, but we must enter into it. It is always there, and when we see it as a comma, a mere pause, we only peek in the door of silence. The ostensible urgency of both the ecological crisis, and of the digital utopias and dystopias that render us distracted, gives us the sense that our silence is a moral indulgence, as though we have no right to enter when there is so much to do and so little time. But hasn't our recent past told the tale of instrumental pragmatism and consumptive competition? And time will tell

---

32. In these words derived from Greek, we encounter compounds; *nous and noia* refer to mind. We contrast their prefixes, meta = with, after; para = beside. Certainly *with* opens us, makes us wonder and receptive. Thinking *with* others and *after* God necessarily quiets us. Thinking *beside* ourselves, self-enclosed, the Cartesian illusion, keeps us from broader learning possibilities. See Laird, *Into the Silent Land*, 10.

33. Legget, *A First Zen Reader*, 130.

the story of our digital frenzied epoch. Our longing for contemplation can be seized by our willing entrance into stillness and silence. *Time willing* is the intentional move from comma . . . to ellipsis. Willing time for silence, sitting still, no surface activity, is a restorative activity of the mind and heart. There is a point when silence may distract our urgent activity, rather than technocratic activity distract our need for silence. Silence calls us; are we listening? The entrance into silence proves a liminal undergoing; we change and we see patterns differently. We hear our heart beating, experience our breath, and view our thoughts. It is like being underwater.

Underwater we can hear less but feel the pulse of our bodies. Being encompassed by water mutes the din of instrumental reason, enveloping us, not unlike solitude. Water too presents us with encounters in thought. Let's move downstream to become opened to, wonder at, receptive of, water. How do we begin to contemplate that of which we are made, that without the consumption of which, we would die?

6

Water and the Erosion
of Instrumental Reason

WATER AS DATUM

MARS HAS HAD WATER, and Jupiter's moon Europa contains ice, and Saturn's moon Titan does have something like petroleum lakes, but by and large, the universe is a pretty dry place compared to the planet earth.[1] Those who search for and speculate about extra-terrestrial life infer from this fact that to find life "out there" in the universe, it is important first to find cosmic water. Planet earth is saturated. On a daily basis we see a fraction of about 1 percent of the water in, with, and above the massive ball we live on. Water is necessary for life as we know it, and that element swirls in and through everything without drawing much attention; unless, of course, we become thirsty or stuck in a hurricane. The hydrological pattern, or cycle, has been sorely compromised due to the patterns of industrialization, which continue unabated. In this context, water becomes perceived mostly as a quantifiable commodity. As data, water is interpreted as little more than an asset in the service of a global economy. Ours is to interrupt the perceptual pattern and interrogate water afresh. Openness, wonder, receptivity, and contemplation serve as solvents for instrumental thinking habits. But first, we understand in order to believe, appreciating water in its quantitative aspect.

1. Perkowitz, "The Six Elements," 209.

Around 97 percent of the earth's water is saline or salt water, 3 percent is fresh water; of that 3 percent, 70 percent is in glaciers. Approximately 30 percent of the fresh water on the earth is ground water and the rest, a fraction of a percent, is in lakes, rivers, and rain, that is, visible parts of the hydrological cycle.[2]

There are at least five serious water issues swirling around this global economy. First, in classical economic terms: it is difficult to get an accurate picture of the supply and demand of water in the coming centuries. There is, however, a projection that, if our consumption practices stay the same, by 2030 there will be a 40 percent gap between the water supply and the demand for water. Secondly, water infrastructure in many places is either old or slip-shod. Quality of delivery is consistently compromised for many reasons, including, but not limited to, corporate abuse of regional water assets. Third, the growth in demand in the next fifty years or so has the potential for political conflict, war, or outright abuses of excluded populations, notably those who are poor. Fourth, many places are presently dehydrated, and have no recourse to public regulations to insure accessibility and infrastructure, which would codify water quality and monitoring.[3] And fifth, to my mind the most pressing, political and technocratic discourse presumes the consumptive paradigm, a device paradigm wrought of industrialization, that which caused the water crisis in the first place. This means we think about water in patterns that have been established, and, like ants rather than human relators, we live in a narrow view of what is possible. Though the planet is saturated, the water necessary for human civilization and survival is small in scale.

Hence, this epoch must work very hard at three things: innovation, sharing resources, and conservation. Instrumental reason is not conducive to the latter two, while innovation has become reduced to taking up old economic and consumptive patterns with new technological precision. What is necessary is to think beyond both technological and market determinism,[4] to engage in smaller scale economies of water infrastructure and to learn water in a new way.

2. Peppard, "Hydrology, Theology and *Laudato Si*," 421.

3. Rao-Monari, "Harnessing the Fourth Industrial Revolution for Water," 5–8.

4. Kerr, "*The Use of Drones*," 1–27.

MORE THAN HYDROGEN AND OXYGEN

First, we can move beyond a strictly scientific vision of what water is. Yes, water can be incisively parsed, broken down to its compound structure. But in doing so we reduce water, we code and name as though water is a thing among other things, like copper or gold, a mere consumptive good. Water isn't. It is unique. Water has the character of repleteness, for it encompasses the globe *and* it is flowing within. Consciousness subsists in water, does it not? Just consider that of which corporeity consists. We are mostly water. Water is *the* consumptive good. In the hierarchy of goods necessary for human flourishing, water is at the top. But after that, it serves as a cultural, spiritual, and pleasurable good. Cities have fountains. Why? It is not utilitarian (except on scorching summer days). It is aesthetic, a symbol of the success of engineering the infrastructure just so, a boast of a cultural kind. Water is a spiritual good. All religious traditions, and specifically Islam, Christianity, and Judaism, interpret water as a gift from the Divine. Water then takes on a sacramental or punitive aspect. In a religious view, water captivates the moral imagination. Water is certainly a useful good. In cooking and healing, in bathing and gardening, water is used to bring together and separate, to cleanse and coagulate. And water is a pleasurable good: in swimming or sunning, in slaking and splashing, in standing out in the rain to cool down; in listening to the gathering storm, in being struck by a deluge. These many ways to encounter water invite us to open our reflection, beyond the pattern of utility and asset, to the edges of the indefinite and replete.

OPENNESS: RESERVOIR IN PLAIN SIGHT

The foregoing discussion of openness, particularly my claim that the open structure sees the openings in structures, applies to human consciousness, but it seems a property of water as well. When flowing, say in a creek, and obstructed by a rock or fallen limb, the flowing water is opened by the obstruction, but, as we will see when we discuss *wonder* below, returns to the given trajectory of its flowing. Water's open structure enables its flow. Malcolm X's imprisoned mind cannot be contained, for it freely flows, investigating the structures that obstruct authentic freedom. His opened mind is free. This is one way we are related to water. Its ubiquity and necessity mean that it becomes a figure in the discovery of meaning; most dynamically water is an analog.

But we can get more specific in relating to water. The open structure of consciousness sees openings because it relates: in anticipation, as co-regulator, as creator of novel patterns. When we apply our relational ways of openness to water, what might we find? Think about how you anticipate water in your life. How do your memory and imagination lead you into encounters with water that stir and convey relational awareness? Swimming through dirty waters? Running through a sprinkler? Coming off the playing field lunging for a drink? Making soup with salt and an ounce of fat? Taking a shower before work/school. Getting ready for a date. Water figures in, and we anticipate our relation to it. How have these relational encounters with water made you a regulator? A participant in water's work? How have you let water function in your daily routines? Now you have tea, now you go to the water fountain, now the bathroom, now the sink. The regular motions of water in our lives are brought to light, brought to the surface. Where will you not drink the water or use the restroom. Why? Is water a necessity before or with dinner? How much water is in my beer, soda, coffee? How necessary are my shower routines? My teeth-brushing, my laundry, dishwashing, gardening routines? What is regular? What *regula* (rule) ought I explore in order to participate responsibly in the work that is water's? What variations in my relation to water ought I consider? Might I begin to test regional waters, to involve myself in new social patterns that align my life with water's healing work? Can I openly discuss my relationship with water with others? How might water be taught to others? Might I consider a water diet, meaning, re-working my patterns of consumption? In my patterns of living, might I re-order these ways so that I am more cognizant of thirst, more aware of quotidian tasks' and habits' reliance on water? The value of water can begin to be measured when we open ourselves to the variable encounters we anticipate, imagine, regulate, and actualize each day. Gratitude could be one of the results, if we are open to it.

WONDER: THE POETICS OF SPLASHES

Leonardo da Vinci studied water and his scientific and poetic sensibilities evoked wonder in water's beauty and properties. He was interested in motion, particularly impetus and percussion. His studies of water's flowing around obstructions give the sense that water has its own telos, what can seem like water's conscious effort or dance. This movement, he thought, is of an infinite variety, and he would drop organic matter in flowing water in order to observe the layered coursings of water's flowing. Leonardo da Vinci studied the way water's flow creates whirlpools, eddies, and vortexes. When the flow is blocked, he observed, water seems to return to the initial angle of its flowing. Water's force then creates an aesthetically pleasing splashing and twirling, almost as if playing in the most exquisite possible form. Leonardo drew these splashes, and noticed that the water's particular bedabbling resembled:

> The behavior of hair, which has two motions, one of which depends on the weight of the strands, the other on the direction of its revolving; thus water makes eddies, one part of which is due to the impetus of the principal current, and the other is due to the incidental motion and flow.[5]

Walter Isaacson would have us notice the analogical at work in da Vinci's observations and sketches. Such a lucid comparison makes us wonder at the intricate structure of nature, and more, it is pleasing to observe both splashes and curls. These analogical observations make us wonder about intrinsic patterns in nature, of which humanity is a small but important part. Initially, da Vinci studied water for engineering purposes, to divert its flow. But the drawings he made of water are, according to Isaacson, evidence of "curiosity about water flow for its own sake."[6] Wonder does that in us: it piques our intelligence toward that which is of interest in and of itself. In this sense, wonder captivates us; we lose ourselves in observation and such loss brings joy, joy in the pursuit of knowledge: the sun setting, an orange ball being submerged by the sea; the vastness of oceans; the pulsing and crashing of waves; the sounds of water, and our mimetic curiosity eager to investigate by sounding the onomatopoeic: kerplunk, drip, splash, etc. The poetic and scientific flirt in wonder. Water is like grace. Both cleanse, both refresh. Grace is like water, both delight and encompass. Eva Saulitis sees in an orca fin an aspergillum, wonder's fruit is the analogy, analogical reasoning not necessarily employed for formal argument, but for the sake of keeping time with the pulse of discovery.

5. Isaacson, *Leonardo da Vinci*, 433.
6. Isaacson, *Leonardo da Vinci*, 432.

RECEPTIVITY: THE TALE OF TWO COKES AND A CUP OF COLD WATER

However, how many of us can be enveloped by an Alaskan Sound? When we are receptive to our surroundings, we may perceive the aged intersection of nature and culture in an infrastructure that is worn down, and, in some places, dangerous. Our water courses through some cities and towns as a solvent that has lost the fight; it now yields a poison solution. Water has been taken over by the very victories of industrialism, the device paradigm that detaches us from machinery, infrastructure, and our own sense of our place in the fabric of rivers, locks, dams, railroads, and highways. Water and its infrastructure, though hidden from view, define every place we walk or drive to.

To receive the truth of the voracious consumerist appetite for water that drives a global economy, it is important to think about our regional dependence on the infrastructure that serves us every day. I live in a city by a bay. A bay-front highway was started in 1989. It connects a major highway to the bay and connects the western and eastern parts of the broader community, which includes suburban sprawl, both east and west. In the summer, when the temperature rises, the bay exudes the smells from its industrial past. On the city's eastern edge of the bay, there is a belching, smoking, coke plant right on the water. Coke is the product that is derived from burning coal at extremely high temperatures. The coke is then used to melt iron at other locations, or used to make phosphorus, which may end up in fertilizers. These furnaces are right on the water, but hidden from bay-front view by a few acres of forest. Just west of the coke plant is the city's sewer processing operation. From both the eastern and western suburban waterworks comes the county's sewage to be processed right on the bay. This is in addition to the city's sewage being carried there. It makes for a humid, hazy, and forebodingly strange smell. Next to the tourist façade of the brightly constructed and alluring shopping sites, those of us who live within the device paradigm are caught off guard by the bay's odors wafting. Matthew Gandy, in his stimulating book *The Fabric of Space,* calls this the "urban uncanny." Sigmund Freud described the discovery of unexpected disorientation as uncanny. And, in Gandy's words, it is "urban dread" that results from the psychological dissonance associated with a "boundary aesthetic," it is disorienting to be exposed to the reality of the populace's eliminations, not to mention industrialism's eco-cidal burping, while shopping for a colorful, plastic, and powerful jet-ski.[7]

Such dread has been fructified by the device paradigm, a pattern that strengthens a detachment: the asymmetry between humanity and reality. Think of what happens when we flush a toilet. Everything is taken care of, out of sight. Is flushing the toilet the precursor to the delete button? Water, and the infrastructure it flows through, takes all manner of waste and washes it away. The waste might as well have not existed, hidden from view, like the coke plant shielded by the trees. I should like to note that the town I live in has a great sewer authority, which does a fine job, and compared to other cities, the water infrastructure is top notch. I am not asking you to be receptive to a critique of failed governance or even residual industrial pollutants, as in Flint, Michigan (though I think the coke plant must go). I am asking you to be receptive to the fact that we can no longer live as though water, and water infrastructure, can be that solvent that keeps us at bay (if you will) from the destructive cultural consumptive habits that will be any city's undoing. From every side of the hydrological cycle, ground to air, to atmosphere and back down again, water has been sorely compromised. The disorienting odors from sewers and industry should rather orient us to a new responsibility. It is time to interrupt the patterns of the device paradigm by way of a renewed focus on water as the place where nature and culture meet. That intersection, so pivotal for the well-being of regions, is taxed by a monstrous complex of global consumption. National and international corporations, scaled to the nth degree, dry up the smaller regional economies, while the waste from their products fill local landfills. Certainly, we're all complicit, but I sense that local infrastructure cannot sustain this rampant consumption in perpetuity.

Globally, it is agriculture that consumes the most fresh water. Not only that, but agricultural run-off has taken its toll on fresh-water lakes. When run-off from farms seeps into the lake, the fertilizer in the run-off over-nourishes the lake's plant life, depleting the oxygen so that the fish and other organisms die. These are a lake's dead zones. Agriculture's fertilizing patterns consistently poison the ecosystem. Whereas agriculture's product is necessary for civilized society,[8] other businesses uses of water seem more abusive. Why? Because on a value scale of goods, certain corporate products

---

7. Gandy, *The Fabric of Space*, 49.

8. Large-scale agribusiness, like other corporations with power and influence, certainly wields its lobbying power and is armed with marketing tools as well.

are certainly not necessary for survival, and may even be detrimental to health. The truth is that the frivolous consumption that drives the global economy wastes the earth's most valuable resource. Though corporate agri-businesses can certainly abuse and deplete the water assets of a region, it is important to distinguish the value of the goods produced. Water used in illegal gold mines, for example, infects water supplies for millions of people, and using valuable water resources for those sorts of operations amounts to a serious breach of human decency.[9]

Though North America has the largest freshwater system in the world in the Great Lakes, the U.S. has been called "the land of Coca-Cola." We might consider what that denomination entails: a land of sugar, corn, cocoa, jolts of high fructose activity, and a tremendously effective history of marketing, branding, and propaganda. In this sense, the cola called Coke does symbolize the U.S.: fertile lands, frenetic activity yielding superficial fun and optimism; a throw-away culture, all packaged and sold elegantly and convincingly. Coke sells "the real thing," coke is "it," with coke you can "taste the feeling." Wow, incredible! Really, just amazing! I hope you can taste the feeling of my sarcasm here.

Coke's global reach is astounding. During World War II, Coke began to find markets by selling the idea that its presence in a nation's economy would enhance that economy by creating new supply chains, notably of sugar.[10] When the nation can supply the sugar and water, the cola company has very cheap assets at its disposal to work with. Highly productive companies, the ones that border on monopolies, find cheap assets and leverage them to sell their product for double or triple what it took to manufacture them. This is good business, of course, this is how the game works, right? But what we need to remember in this global context is that the Coca-Cola company has made its fortunes from the water infrastructures that *serve* the *public* good. As recently as 2004, in Tamil Nadu, India, Coke had a plant in a secluded village, and, according to villagers, "the plant sucked their wells dry and polluted their streams."[11] Finding water sources for sugary drinks that result in diabetes, utilize the plastic-bottling process, create a throw-away waste that ends up in the oceans, all the while developing a bottled water wing of the business, takes an audacious corporate will as well as well-formed and addicted customers. It also seems to take a good bit of

9. Negro Chin, "Dirty Rivers," 18.
10. Elmore, *Citizen Coke*, 157.
11. Elmore, *Citizen Coke*, 155.

denial. The whole world has been hosed by Coke. How much denial are we in here? I ask this question because Coke is the business paradigm for consumptive economies, which keep us addicted to convenience, efficiency, and what is superficial. The telecommunications act of 1996 opened media companies to the public utilities that had been bought and paid for by taxpayers and what became AT&T, a public-utilities project.[12] Multi-national companies have a history of hidden assets that were originally structured for common goods. Assets intended for all are gobbled up by the few, and in the case of Coke, fresh drinking water is abused, and sold back to the customer as a tooth-decaying stimulant.

How much water could be shared instead of the water going into producing that *one* caramelly-looking sexy bottle? Coke is not real, and it is not what "it" is (to negate a common saying, *it is what it is*, p is p). Let us just be receptive to the facts though. That will help us to analyze the problem before us. As has been mentioned, Coke came of age in the progressive era, when it took advantage of public utilities and the public-health mandate of access to clean water. At the end of the twentieth century, coke would use seventy-nine billion gallons of water annually to dilute its syrup. However, importantly, that seventy-nine billion is only 1% of Coke's total water footprint, a calculation based on bottling, supply chains, and water used in agriculture for the product. That amounts to eight trillion gallons per year. According to Bartow Elmore, the amount of water Coke uses in a year could "meet the annual cooking, cleaning, and drinking needs of over 2 billion people, or close to a quarter of the world's population."[13] Now, think about other international bottling operations, large-scale beer companies, for example. Consumptive economies' habitual thirst is an immoral corporate indulgence pattern, something we buy into with a smile of denial. There are many places in the world that don't have access to quality water resources. The early twentieth century's moral intentions motivating infrastructure, the universal right to good water, have largely been forgotten. Yet, I can remember all the Coke slogans from my childhood, here is a doozy: coke adds life. We have shown the opposite to be the case: Coke depletes life. And it's not just Coke, of course, for Coke has become a symbol of the chronic business of depleting the earth's resources while benefitting the few, the comfortable. If, as a person of faith, I take Jesus' words seriously, I am called to be receptive to his prophetic and tender mandate from Matthew 10:41–42:

12 Nuechterlein, *Digital Crossroads*, 16–19.

13. Elmore, *Citizen Coke*, 17–18.

> Anyone who receives a prophet because he is a prophet will receive
> a prophet's reward, and anyone who receives a righteous man be-
> cause he is a righteous man will receive a righteous man's reward.
> And if anyone gives even a cup of cold water to one of these little
> ones because he is my disciple, I tell you the truth, he will certainly
> not lose his reward.

As people of faith we stand between global corporate power and the little ones. Inhabiting this place, we encounter that integration of incisive critique and gentle truth. Called to be receptive to both, we are invited to see with God the simple elegance of sharing the gift of water, for many are thirsty.

CONTEMPLATION: BEYOND THE LOCK, THE DAM

The ancient text from Matthew cajoles our moral imagination. It is the end of Jesus' instructions to the twelve apostles as they prepare to go out to battle evil and to heal every sickness. He seems to give them a map of their possible encounters. You may be received, or not received; you may speak the truth in prophecy, or you may simply be a righteous person among others. The other possibility is simply to care for people in need. Not too flashy or exciting, it may not bring the historical fame of martyrdom or the great repute of the magnanimous person. But the simplicity of the action of offering the life-sustaining element to all manner of poor, the ones who must always live in the mode of survival; is that not something each of us can accomplish, can pursue? And we understand, with Jesus, what the exhilaration of slaking thirst in the scorching heat really means in the mind of God: someone God loves is encountered, received, cared for, and refreshed. Offering to share a cup of cold water is elementary, a basis for all other moral behavior. And water is the basis for all other growth and nourishment. Sharing is elemental to the moral life; water is elemental to all life. Sharing elements with one another confirms our shared humanity. Air is the same way, as is soil. We share these elements in ways that form the foundation of all other kinds of sharing. The lake that forms the bay in the city where I live stretches all the way to Cleveland and beyond. The suburban development in each direction, east and west and south, relies on the same water that the city enjoys, though the tax boundaries are a social construct through which urban and suburban identity can be named, shaped, and perpetuated. But the same water, and sewage infrastructure, serves these bounded identities. As an elemental entity, water has no such boundaries. Our common and innate need of fresh water means we are the same: human beings reliant on a vast network of concrete, steel, and copper to divert water's elemental flow into our cups and into our mouths. Though we socially construct identities; white, Indian, African American, immigrant, rich, poor, suburban, urban, an elemental like water cannot facilitate nor confirm these ostentatious categories. When we think about the vegetables plated next to the steak at a five-star restaurant, we realize they grew in the same soil we all share, the soil the cow who is now the steak shat upon. When we think about the air I intake as I scream at the referee at my son's basketball game, or argue vociferously with the city councilman, it is the same air that I, the ref, the city councilman need. If I could find a way to take the air from my enemy and leverage it for my benefit alone, would I?

Air, earth, water, these are not things. They resist being possessed like things, mined like things, manipulated like things, treated like things. Unlike things, they don't disappear, or dissipate because they have been abused, polluted, cut into. The elementals carry on with the poisons, the wounds. For these elementals are bound and determined by the earth's physical complex and inter-connected structures, but more, they are the substance of those orders and patterns. They may seem to us sick, but they are not going away, unlike creatures. We are what is sick; elementals do not get sick; they persist. Contemplating the meaning of water, the meaning of sharing our common humanity in an elemental way, involves a return of that sense of being encompassed. Though we can divert waters' flow, who can stand inside a storm and perceive each side of its envelopment? A return to the elemental as distinct from things means that we are enticed to recapitulate our interpretive capacities. Things are trees, corn, rocks, fish, skyscrapers, baseballs. These are things. Elementals they are not. Elementals encompass all these things. When it is raining, to what does the "it" refer? The elementals are less distinctively individualized, less readily objectified, indefinite. Unlike a tree, a storm is not an object.[14] When introduced to the history of philosophy as a distinct and disciplined use of reason in order to discover, for example, why there is something rather than nothing, students meet the pre-Socratic philosophers who made claims for the most significant elements. Thales thought it water, Anaximenes, a half-century later, claimed it to be air. In addition to offering to students an evocative question regarding the persistence and nature of the elements, we point out that different scientists give priority to different elements. Another aspect

14. Sallis, "The Elemental Turn," 348–49.

also shows itself to be interesting. The elementals combine in different proportions, varying degrees of dynamism. For example, ocean foam is made of air and water.[15] These contemplatives, the first scientists, I want to note well, discerned a scale of value as they named the elements. One gave water first place, one air. To our point: contemplation is an egress through which we pass over the mundane patterns that confine the mind to receive a deep sense of significance and profound value. Thus, when we think with the elemental, water is sensed in its indispensable worth and givenness.

THE CONFLUENCE OF INTELLECTUAL AND REGIONAL VIRTUE

When we are disposed, or even predisposed, to openness, wonder, receptivity, and contemplation, we become focused more intentionally on our surroundings. We double down on daily engagements, focal practices, and the region: neighborhood, block, house, family, person—the manifold context that both elicits and impinges on our freedom. We measure national debates, political rhetoric, digital images, commercials, and social media by our sense of place, the stimulating happenstance of our unique existence. Circumstance takes precedence. We see reality more accurately when we learn to see beyond the buzz of frenetic communication toward whatever is at hand. The result is a deeper sense of responsibility to our surroundings: water, earth, wind, litter, infrastructure, engagement. Living without, living within, we assemble encounters of thought that enliven authenticity. The regional takes first place in our awareness. The standards set by the markets of technocracy; efficient solutions to manage commerce, the environment, healthcare, education, criminal justice, politics, even religion; all these can distract us from the encounter with that which encompasses us. If we live solely through technocracy we will lose, to varying degrees, our capacity to freely analyze and create. What we have shown in the foregoing essay is that, for the most part, the digitization of culture, for all its benefits, is simply another version of mindless conformity. Patterns set by the technological paradigm work against human freedom all the while detaching us from one another and nature. Thankfully, we have innate capacities, given by the Creator, through which we can interrupt these patterns and order our lives in conformity with the structure of our consciousness. It is a structure built for the love of discovery, that which flows to truth.

15. Perkowitz, "The Six Elements," 209.

Epilogue
Allegory of the Keg (After Plato)

ALL AROUND THE STEEL cylinder, pumping the tube, the students stand, wait, and assume the position of consumers. Standard coils connect all to the keg. The data flows from water infused with barley and hops, straight to their heads it goes, and then it happens: awareness. Cognition curves from their shadows, now amplified by sampled draughts of reason. Suddenly, softly, no one is agnostic, or, everyone falls into line, to learn aggregations, the many ways to consume keg, the chemistry of the contents, the shapes and configurations it could take, how it may be made even easier to swallow or see. The reason of their consumption counts for so much different knowledge. Answers to so many questions traverse the tools commodiously, ending up in the stomach of the soul, chambered somewhere in the grid of understanding. So many ways to figure for X-preferences, factors in the reasons for standing at the keg, bound to premonitions of self-hood. Those students whose major discipline mirrors the movements of the keg are the professed; the farther out the tubes stretch, the more abstract knowledge of the keg becomes, but all must take the taste test no matter the angle of their learning, and all will pass with vying colors. This is the way things are, the preferential option for making sound judgments, becoming of a cunning consumer. The keg room is the only known surface by which cognition flattens out, inebriated in time with the standard coil. So, knowing goings on, scrolling through made-by-self lives, striving for plans to insure unambiguous experiences of self-evident preferences (premises); each to his own tubular connection to the keg. Heads are up when heads are down calibrating keg work, studying sounds from the keg's manifold—the sound of knowledge is keg aspiration, datum upon datum, whips of what is cool, or hot, clicks from taps, and cliques sounding off to keg-master who has got

Jobs galore. The tappers of keg are an efficient lot, hard to see, but easy to
spot due to the absence of their soft skills. Soft skills are good for keeping
your place in the keg room, nothing more really, and for trading echoes of
self-understanding. The keg room is what counts, for real. Now in the keg
room two students accidently heard stranger sounds—not taps, nor chambered echoes, not clicks, nor scrolling aspirations. It's the sound of leaking
liquid, unheard of in the history of the keg's standard coil. It is their tubes,
their connections more than severed, unhinged. They hear only taps and
empty cackles, they see no shapes, nor forms, they are alert in an unkempt
room, their tubes and tapestries of the coil broken clean off, drawing no
more drafts. They are dizzy; a spinning array of perceptions befall them. No
longer tethered to the keg, they see the boundaries of the room, its sticky
substructure, and peering around, all the connected learners, crawling at
consuming information. They follow the sound of the leaking tubes to a
threshold, an open door that appears as a flag, a-wisp from chance winds.
Through the door appear three freshwater streams, unencumbered by
tubes, coiling as if to play, forming a confluence of clear water. Cupping
their hands, they drink. Thereby their thirst was discovered at the point it
was slaked, the release of reason. A deeper hue of orientation fixated and
straightened their cognitive curves. Beyond the confluence they beheld
unused maths, virgin psychologies, and topoi that had indeterminate prefixes, theirs to grasp and name. The trees were something other than wood,
the dirt clean. Rocks and ridges tabulated their movements. Time was not
theirs, nor was it noticed, for they were lost moment by moment in the
foundry of reason. There they saw each other, amplified not by preferences,
nor profession, nor by anything standard coil could assess or enhance. They
were there listening hard to each other in silence . . . concentrating with
the ease of their growing grins. A third lent time to the moment, a novel
we it was. We was never so singular, so alive, so present sensed. When they
spoke, the sound traveled farther than they could ever remember and they
paused to wait for the din to return to their ideas. They peeled ideas slowly,
so as not to tear the thoughts, for they understood just then that thoughts
too have cuticles. "I am never going back to the keg room," said one. "If I
knew then what I now know, I would have left a long time ago." The other
one asked, "I feel for all our friends in the keg room, don't you?" "Yes I do."
Walking along the river banks for a long time, they came to the door again.
"I think everyone deserves to come to the river." One replied, "Will we be
thought strange and out of touch?" The other one put her hand on the door,

"Yes, but we can talk about the dirt, the trees, the ridges, and everything, to bring others to see what we have seen, to discover, to enter the novelty, the novel we." And so it is the duty of those who have left the keg to risk misunderstanding and derision to walk with the kegged, to invite them to meet the sound of rushing, clean, clear water, and to drink. For in that very risk, they will be liberated from standard coil, discovering their thirst for reason.

Bibliography

Anselm. *Proslogion, Monologium and Cur Deus Homo*. Translated by Sydney Norton Deane. Lasalle, IL: Open Court, 1948.

Aristotle. *Basic Works*. Edited by Richard McKeon. New York: Random House, 1941.

———. *Nicomachean Ethics*. Translated by Robert C. Bartlett and Susan D. Collins. Chicago: University of Chicago Press, 2011.

———. *Poetics*. Translated, with an introduction and notes by Malcolm Heath. London: Penguin, 1996.

———. *The Works of Aristotle Translated into English*. Translated by J. A. Smith and W. D. Ross. Vols. 4 and 5. Oxford: Clarendon, 1910.

Saint Augustine. *Confessions*. Translated by Henry Chadwick. Oxford: Oxford University Press, 1991.

Bishop, Jeffrey. *The Anticipatory Corpse: Medicine, Power and the Care of the Dying*. Notre Dame, IN: University of Notre Dame Press, 2011.

Borgmann, Albert. *Crossing the Postmodern Divide*. Chicago: University of Chicago Press, 1992.

———. "Digital Restlessness and Something More Certain." *Comment Magazine*, Summer 34.2 (2016) 26–31.

———. *Holding on to Reality: The Nature of Information at the Turn of the Millennium*. Chicago: University of Chicago Press, 2000.

———. "Information, Nearness and Farness." In *The Robot in the Garden: Tele-robotics and Tel-epistemology in the Age of the Internet*, edited by Ken Goldberg, 91–107. Cambridge: MIT Press, 2001.

———. "Reflections and Reviews: The Moral Complexion of Consumption." *Journal of Consumer Research* 26 (2000) 418–22.

———. *Technology and the Character of Contemporary Life: A Philosophical Inquiry*. Chicago: University of Chicago Press, 1984.

Bruni, Luigino, and Stefano Zamagni. *Civil Economy*. Newcastle upon Tyne, UK: Agenda, 2016.

Buber, Martin. *I and Thou*. Translated by Ronald Gregor Smith. New York: Scribners, 1958.

———. *Tales of the Hasidim*. Translated by Olga Marx. New York: Schocken, 1975.

Byl, Christine. "Every Reason to Stay: Eva Saulitis's Life with Whales." *The Sun,* Jan 2017, 6–13.

Diangelo, Robin. "White Fragility." *International Journal of Critical Pedagogy* 3 (2011) 54–70.

Eadmer. *The Life of St Anselm*. Edited and Translated by R. W. Southern. New York: Thomas Nelson, 1962.

Elmore, Bartow J. *Citizen Coke: The Making of Coca-Cola Capitalism*. New York: Norton, 2015.

Farley, Edward. *Deep Symbols: Their Postmodern Effacement and Reclamation*. Valley Forge, PA: Trinity, 1996.

Fuller, Robert C. *Wonder: From Emotion to Spirituality*. Chapel Hill, NC: University of North Carolina Press, 2006.

Gandy, Matthew. *The Fabric of Space: Water Modernity, and the Urban Imagination*. Cambridge: MIT Press, 2014.

Gilson, Etienne. *The Unity of Philosophical Experience*. New York: Scribners, 1937.

Gaál Gyulai, Emery de. *The Art of Equanimity: A Study on the Theological Hermeneutics of Saint Anselm of Canterbury*. Bern: Peter Lang, 2002.

Goodman, Leslee. "Quiet Please: Gordon Hempton and the Search for Silence." *The Sun*, Sept 2010, 5–12.

Gros, Frédéric. *A Philosophy of Walking*. Translated by John Howe. London: Verso, 2014.

Issacson, Walter. *Leonardo Da Vinci*. New York: Simon and Schuster, 2017.

Jaeger, Werner. *Aristotle: Fundamentals of the History of His Development*. Translated by Richard Robinson. 2nd ed. Oxford: Clarendon, 1948.

Heschel, Abraham Joshua. *The Sabbath*. New York: Farrar, Straus and Giroux, 1951.

Heschel, Abraham Joshua, and Samuel H. Dresner. *I Asked for Wonder: A Spiritual Anthology*. New York: Crossroad, 1983.

Hudson, Robert. *The Monk's Record Player: Thomas Merton, Bob Dylan, and the Perilous Summer of 1966*. Grand Rapids: Eerdmans, 2018.

Keating, Thomas. *Open Mind Open Heart: The Contemplative Dimension of the Gospel*. New York: Continuum, 2002.

Kerr, Aaron. "Borgmann on Merton." *Logos: A Journal of Catholic Thought and Culture* 19.1 (2016) 57–78.

———. "The Use of Drones: An Argument against Optimistic Technological Determinism Featuring the Work of Albert Borgmann and an Extended Analogy." *Humanities and Technology Review* 34 (2015) 1–33.

Kerr, Fergus. *Theology After Wittgenstein*. Oxford: Blackwell, 1986.

Kahn, Charles. *The Art and Thought of Heraclitus*. London: Cambridge, 1979.

Laird, Martin, O.S.A. *Into the Silent Land: A Guide to the Christian Practice of Contemplation*. New York: Oxford University Press, 2006.

LeClercq, Jean, O.S.B. "New Forms of Contemplative Life." *Theological Studies* 33.2 (1972) 307–19.

Leggett, Trevor. *A First Zen Reader*. Rutland, VT: Tuttle, 1981.

Marable Manning, William. *Malcolm X: A Life of Reinvention*. New York: Viking, 2011.

Marcel, Gabriel. *The Mystery of Being, Vol. II: Faith and Reality*. Translated by G. S. Fraser. South Bend, IN: St Augustine's, 2001.

Martinez "The Readings of a Diarist: Thomas Merton as a Reader of Journals and Related Works (Part II)." *Cistercian Studies Quarterly* 50.3 (2015) 320–69.

Merton, Thomas. *The Asian Journal of Thomas Merton*. Edited by Naomi Burton, Brother Patrick Hart, and James Laughlin. New York: New Directions, 1973.

———. *Cistercian Fathers and Forefathers: Essays and Conferences*. Edited by Patrick F. O'Connell. New York: New City, 2018.

————. *Entering the Silence: Becoming a Monk and Writer*. Edited by Jonathan Montaldo. San Francisco: Harper Collins, 1995.

————. *Faith and Violence: Christian Teaching and Christian Practice*. Notre Dame, IN: University of Notre Dame Press, 1968.

————. *New Seeds of Contemplation*. New York: New Directions, 1961.

————. *Passion for Peace: The Social Essays*. Edited by William H. Shannon. New York: Crossroad, 1995.

————. *Selected Essays*. Edited by Patrick F. O'Connell. Maryknoll, NY: Orbis, 2013.

National Park Service. "Conservation vs. Preservation and the National Park Service." https://www.nps.gov/klgo/learn/education/classrooms/conservation-vs-preservation.htm.

Nuechterlein, Jonathan E., and Philip J. Weiser. *Digital Crossroads: Telecommunications, Law and Policy in the Internet Age*. Cambridge: MIT Press, 2013.

Negro Chin, Maria-Pia. "Dirty Rivers." *Maryknoll Magazine*, July/August 2017, 12–16.

Niebuhr, Helmut Richard. *The Responsible Self: An Essay in Christian Moral Philosophy*. San Francisco: Harper & Row, 1978.

Noddings, Nel. *Caring: A Feminist Approach to Ethics and Moral Education*. Berkeley: University of California Press, 1984.

————. *Philosophy of Education*. Boulder, CO: Westview, 2012.

O'Connell, Patrick F. "From Lectio to Lyric: Thomas Merton's Early Poetry on Biblical Narratives." *Cistercian Quarterly* 52.3 (2017) 311–45.

————, ed. *The Vision of Thomas Merton*. Notre Dame, IN: Ave Maria, 2003.

Peppard, Christiana. "Hydrology, Theology, and *Laudato Si*." *Theological Studies* 77 (2016) 416–35.

Perkowitz, Sydney. "The Six Elements: Visions of a Complex Universe." *Leonardo* 43 (2010) 208–11.

Plato. *The Republic*. Translated by Francis McDonald Cornford. New York: Oxford University Press, 1945.

Pope Francis. "*Laudato Si: On Care for Our Common Home*." http://w2.vatican.va/content/francesco/en/encyclicals/documents/papa-francesco_20150524_enciclica-laudato-si.html.

Rao-Monari, Usha, and Dominic Waughray. "Harnessing the Fourth Industrial Revolution for Water." *World Economic Forum*. https://www.weforum.org/reports/harnessing-the-fourth-industrial-revolution-for-water.

Reichmann, James, S.J. *Philosophy of the Human Person*. Chicago: Loyola University Press, 1985.

Rossmanith, Nicole, and Vasudevi Reddy. "Structure and Openness in the Development of Self in Infancy." *Journal of Consciousness Studies* 23 (2016) 237–57.

Sallis, John. "The Elemental Turn." *The Southern Journal of Philosophy* 50.2 (2012) 345–50.

Saulitis, Eva. *Becoming Earth*. Pasadena, CA: Boreal, 2016.

————. *Into Great Silence*. Boston: Beacon, 2013.

Schumacher, E .F. *A Guide for the Perplexed*. New York: Harper and Row, 1977.

Shaughnessy, Michael F. "Features, An Interview with Richard Louv: About Nature-Deficit Disorder." *Taproot Journal* 15.2 (2005) 4–5.

Slote, Michael. *From Enlightenment to Receptivity: Rethinking our Values*. New York: Oxford University Press, 2013.

Sokolowski, Robert. *Introduction to Phenomenology*. Cambridge: Cambridge University Press, 1999.

————. *Presence and Absence: A Philosophical Investigation of Language and Being.* Bloomington, IN: Indiana University Press, 1978.

Southern, R. W. *St Anselm: A Portrait in a Landscape.* New York: Cambridge University Press, 1990.

Steingraber, Sandra. *Living Downstream: An Ecologist's Personal Investigation of Cancer and the Environment.* Cambridge, MA: DeCapo, 2010.

Tracy, David. *The Analogical Imagination.* New York: Crossroad, 1981.

Voegelin, Eric. "The Meditative Origin of the Philosophical Knowledge of Order." In *The Beginning and Beyond: Papers from the Gadamer and Voegelin Conferences,* edited by Fred Lawrence, 43–51. Chico, CA: Scholars, 1984.

Tuan, Yi-Fu. *Space and Place: The Perspective of Experience.* Minneapolis: University of Minnesota Press, 1977.

Twenge, Jean M. "Have Smartphones Destroyed a Generation?" *The Atlantic Monthly,* September 2017. https://www.theatlantic.com/magazine/archive/2017/09/has-the-smartphone-destroyed-a-generation/534198/.

Walker, Michelle Boulous. *Slow Philosophy: Reading Against the Institution.* London: Bloomsbury, 2017.

Wittgenstein, Ludwig. *Tractatus Logico-Philosophicus.* Translated by D. F. Pears and B. F. McGuiness. New York: Routledge, 1964.

Whitehead, Alfred North. *Adventures of Ideas.* New York: McMillan, 1933.

X, Malcolm. *The Autobiography of Malcolm X as Told to Alex Haley.* New York: Ballantine Books, 1965.

————. *The Last Speeches.* Edited by Bruce Perry. New York: Pathfinder, 1989.

————. *Malcolm X Speaks.* Edited by George Breitman. New York: Pathfinder, 1989.

Zagzebski, Linda Trinkaus. "Exemplarist Virtue Theory." *Metaphilosophy* 41(2010) 41–57.

————. *Philosophy of Religion: An Historical Introduction.* Malden, MA: Blackwell, 2007.

————. *Virtues of the Mind: An Inquiry into the Nature of Virtue and the Ethical Foundations of Knowledge.* New York: Cambridge University Press, 1996.

Index

Index

Made in the USA
Monee, IL
13 January 2020